TEXAS
HISTORY
for Kids

Lone Star Lives and Legends

WITH 21 ACTIVITIES

Karen Bush Gibson

CHICAGO
REVIEW
PRESS

Published by Chicago Review Press Incorporated
814 North Franklin Street
Chicago, Illinois 60610
ISBN 978-1-61374-989-0

Library of Congress Cataloging-in-Publication Data
Gibson, Karen Bush.
  Texas history for kids : Lone Star lives and legends, with 21 activities / Karen Bush Gibson. —
First edition.
    pages cm
  Includes bibliographical references and index.
  ISBN 978-1-61374-989-0 (trade paper)
  1. Texas—History—Juvenile literature. I. Title.

F386.3.G53 2015
976.4—dc23

                                                2014031088

Cover and interior design: Monica Baziuk
Interior illustrations: Jim Spence
Cover images: Front, counterclockwise: Alamo, iStock © Augustine Change; Heywood #2
gusher, LOC; folkloric dancer, Shutterstock © Jeff Schultes; astronaut, iStock © Purdue9394;
Battle of the Alamo, LOC. Back, from top: Hurricane of 1900 wreckage, LOC; Samuel Houston,
LOC; Mission Concepción, Karen Bush Gibson.

Printed in the United States of America
5 4 3

To Ray and Betty Bush
for introducing me to Texas
and being such amazing parents

Contents

Time Line

248 million years ago

Mesozoic Era begins. This includes the Cretaceous Period.

11,200 years ago

Paleo-Indians migrate to Texas

1519 Alonso Álvarez de Pineda sails the Texas coast and creates the first map

1528 Álvar Núñez Cabeza de Vaca is the first known European in Texas

1541 Franciso Vásquez de Coronado explores the Southwest in search for gold; discovers Palo Duro Canyon

1632 The first mission is established in San Angelo; it lasts for six months

1684 Franciscan missionaries begin establishing missions throughout Texas

1685 René-Robert Cavelier, Sieur de La Salle, lands at Matagorda Bay and establishes a French settlement, Fort St. Louis

1700 The Comanche acquire horses from the Spanish

Mission San Francisco de Solano is established near the Rio Grande; it is later moved to San Antonio and renamed San Antonio de Valero

1724 San Antonio de Valero mission moves to the east bank of the San Antonio River; this site will later be called the Alamo

1817 Pirate Jean Lafitte establishes a colony on Galveston Island

1821 Mexico wins independence from Spain

First colonists arrive at Stephen Austin's settlement

OKLAHOMA

•Tulsa

•Santa Fe

⊕Oklahoma City

⊕Albuquerque

ARKANSAS

•Amarillo
Palo Duro Canyon

NEW MEXICO

Red River

•Shreveport

•Lubbock

Fort Worth •Dallas
Dinosaur Valley State Park •Arlington

•Corsicana

Nacogdoches•

El Paso•

•Midland

TEXAS

Pecos River

Paluxey River

Brazos River

Canadian River

Alabama-Coushatta Reservation

Buttermilk Creek

•Fredericksburg Austin⊕

Guadalupe River

Colorado River

•Beaumont Orange•

Sabine Pass

Seminole Canyon State Park

Boerne• New Braunfels•

•Gonzales

Houston•

San Antonio •

•Goliad

•Galveston

Matagorda Bay

MEXICO

Rio Grande River

Corpus Christi•

Padre Island

•Laredo

Gulf of Mexico

Laguna Madre

Rio Grande River

•Brownsville

100 miles

Introduction

How do you explain Texas to someone who has never been there? Do you talk about the Wild West qualities or the modern cities of steel and glass erupting from the plains? Is Texas the mesas, plateaus, and desert valleys of West Texas? The long line of beaches, islands, and marshes along the coast? Or the gently rolling land of Hill Country, or the Piney Woods of East Texas?

You can ask the same about the people—cowboys, oilmen, strong women, Latinos, or technology geniuses. Like many states, the area today known as Texas has been ruled and influenced by many countries and cultures—Spanish, Mexican, French, German, Czech, and more. Each left its mark.

Texas is many things to many people.

Texas is a huge state—268,820 square miles—and probably has the most recognizable shape on the map.

That area covers a variety of geographical terrains and people.

But Texas is also an attitude. Texans like to brag that they do things big in the Lone Star State. That includes the history. From the early dinosaurs to flying in space, Texas delights in the stories of its land and people.

For years, a story has circulated that Texans were quite upset at losing the distinction of being the largest state in the Union when Alaska was admitted as a state in 1959. Alaska, at over twice the size of Texas, was upstaging Texas, and that just would not do. The story says that some Texans got together and joked about melting Alaska.

Texas has a population of over 26 million people, coming in second to California. But Texans have more room to move around with 96.3 people per square mile; California has to fit 239.1 people into the same area.

Author John Steinbeck may have said it best in *Travels with Charley* (1962): "I have said that Texas is a state of mind, but I think it is more than that. It is a mystique closely approximating a religion.... Texas is the obsession, the proper study, and the passionate possession of all Texans."

★ Texas Fast Facts

Capital: Austin

State Nickname: The Lone Star State

State Motto: Friendship

Entered Union: December 29, 1845

Population (2012 estimate): 26,059,203

Percentage of population under 18 years old (2012): 26.8

Total Land Area: 268,201 square miles

Length of Coastline: 367 miles (tidal shoreline 3,359 miles)

Highest Point: Guadalupe Peak, 8,751 feet

Lowest Point: 0 feet, where the Rio Grande meets the Gulf of Mexico

Largest City: Houston (fourth largest in United States)

Second Largest City: San Antonio

National Park Acreage: 8,618 acres

Official State Flower: Bluebonnet

Official Mammal: Longhorn

Official State Dish: Chili

First Word Spoken on the Moon: Houston

Number of Amusement Parks: 12

Number of Oil Wells: 832

Average Number of Tornados Each Year: 139 (more than any other state)

How Often Hurricanes Strike the Texas Coast: Roughly once every 9 to 16 years

Cretaceous Times

The sun was shining upon Glen Rose, in the north central part of Texas. It was the kind of day made for being outdoors. And that's just where nine-year-old George Adams was. Instead of going to school one day in 1909, George decided to go exploring at the nearby Wheeler Branch Creek, which was part of the Paluxey River. George probably scanned the ground for interesting bugs and tested himself by throwing rocks toward the other side of the creek.

Tracks found in Dinosaur Valley State Park.

George stopped what he was doing as soon as he saw something strange in the shallow clear water—the tracks of a large animal with three toes on each foot. It looked like the tracks of a giant bird. George was interested, and a little scared. He ran to school to tell his teacher and principal what he found. The school had an impromptu field trip to see the tracks.

They weren't the only people to see the tracks at the Paluxy. The river was also popular with moonshiners like Charlie Moss, who was scouting locations to set up a still to brew illegal liquor when he came across the tracks.

Southern Methodist University paleontologist Dr. Ellis Shuler identified the tracks as belonging to a theropod dinosaur, one that primarily traveled on two feet. Dr. Shuler published a paper about the tracks in 1918. Afterward, the tracks were largely forgotten, although replicas were made and sold at tourist stops throughout the Southwest. That's where fossil collector R. T. Bird saw the theropod tracks, at a trading post in Gallup, New Mexico. Bird, who worked for the American Museum of Natural History in New York, thought the tracks showed amazing detail. He decided to return to New York through Glen Rose, Texas.

The actual tracks were even more impressive. Bird believed that they probably belonged to the Acrocanthosaurus, a smaller relative of Tyrannosaurus rex. The tracks ranged from 12 to 24 inches long and 9 to 17 inches wide. And there were more. Bird was able to uncover more of the trackway, a collection of the footprints as the dinosaur moved.

While looking for more theropod tracks, Bird came upon a print that looked like an elephant track. But it wasn't; it belonged to a sauropod. Not only was it the first he had ever seen, it was also one of the clearest prints anyone had ever found of the four-legged dinosaurs.

Upon further investigation, Bird discovered a trackway with prints from multiple dinosaurs, both sauropods and theropods. Bird's theory was that the smaller, carnivorous theropods were chasing the larger plant-eating sauropods. Sauropods traveled in herds with the adults on the outside and the youth in the middle. Moving only 2.7 miles an hour, they needed to use size to their advantage to escape the faster theropods traveling 5 miles an hour.

Although Glen Rose is located in the Paluxy River Valley where evergreen woodlands and prairie grasses cover the terrain, it hadn't always looked like this. During the Cretaceous period, Glen Rose was on the Texas coast, and a shallow sea covered the area. The shells of crustaceans left the area rich in limestone, so the dinosaurs left their tracks in calcium-rich mud.

Twenty-one of the 300 known dinosaur species lived in what is now Texas. Discoveries made so far suggest that dinosaurs first

ACTIVITY
Plaster Cast Tracks

People can learn a lot from the tracks they see on the ground. Look around for animal tracks in a place where the soil is damp. Make your own plaster cast track, just like the professionals do.

Materials
★ Paper towels
★ Hairspray or spray lacquer
★ Scrap cardboard
★ 1 pint water in a plastic bottle
★ 1 pound plaster of paris in a large strong plastic ziplock bag
★ Stick or ruler
★ Small trowel or spade
★ Old toothbrush
★ Newspaper or bubble wrap

1. Carefully clear away any small rocks or loose soil from around the edge of the track. Soak up any excess water by dipping a paper towel into the water. If your track is in loose soil or sand, try spraying it with hairspray first to hold the soil together better while you're making the cast.

2. Make a border or wall around the track with the cardboard.

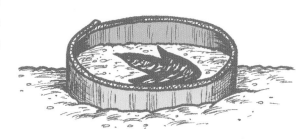

3. Pour half of the bottle of water into the plastic bag of plaster. Seal the ziplock and mix by kneading through the bag to get a smooth and even consistency. Add more water if needed.

4. After the plaster of paris is mixed, cut the bag in one bottom corner. You can squeeze the plaster through the hole onto the track. Pour from one side and let it flow into the track.

5. Tap the surface of the wet cast with a stick or ruler to release any air bubbles.

6. After about 30 minutes once the plaster is totally dry, use the spade or trowel to lift it from the ground. If you make a large plaster cast, it may take longer to dry. Dig a few inches away from the cast.

7. Allow the removed cast to dry overnight before trying to remove any soil left on the bottom of the cast. When you do remove excess soil, use an old toothbrush.

8. Spray with hairspray or lacquer to strengthen the mark and prevent it from crumbling during handling.

9. Wrap the cast in newspaper or bubble wrap to protect it from damage.

appeared in the late Triassic period before flourishing in the Cretaceous period. The tracks at Glen Rose became Dinosaur Valley State Park, and people come from around the world to see them.

About 113 million years ago limestone, sandstone, and mudstone was deposited along the shoreline of an ancient sea. Over the last million years, the river has sculpted the rock and worn it down to reveal large amounts of rocky ground on the river bottom.

Upriver from Dinosaur Valley State Park, the paleontology department from Southern Methodist University was at work on dinosaur bones found at a ranch in 2007. Graduate student Peter Rose had never seen anything like them. At 60 to 70 feet long and 12 feet high, the 20-ton dinosaur had a long neck, even longer than its tail. Interestingly, its footprints matched those of the sauropod tracks in Glen Rose. The dinosaur was named the *Paluxysaurus jonesi* in 2007 and designated the Texas state dinosaur two years later.

Prehistoric Animals

ABOUT 65 million years ago, the dinosaurs disappeared. A giant meteor hit the Earth so hard that tidal waves traveled inland at least 150 miles from the coast, depositing treasures from the sea in the Brazos River area. Mammoths, giant armadillos, and other prehistoric mammals replaced the dinosaurs.

Both dinosaurs and prehistoric mammals left behind bones, fossils, and tracks that can be seen at museums throughout the world. In recent years, the Houston Museum of Natural History and the Perot Museum of Nature and Science in Dallas have joined the world's museums in showcasing the early prehistory of Texas.

In 1989, 12-year-old Johnny Maurice and his father were looking for shark's teeth in the yellow-gray shallow mud near Fort Worth. The

★ Dinosaur Valley State Park

Dinosaur Valley State Park opened in 1972, though it had been designated a National Natural Landmark by the National Park Service in 1968. Located just northwest of Glen Rose on the Paluxy River, the park covers approximately 1,524 acres. In addition to the tracks in the riverbed, visitors can see dinosaur models from the 1964 World's Fair in New York City—a 70-foot Apatosaurus and a 45-foot Tyrannosaurus rex. Over 200,000 visitors enjoy the park each year.

A full-scale dinosaur statue in Glen Rose Dino Park.

From Texas With Love, Wikimedia Commons

region was once a marine area, and fossilized remains of marine animals have been found there by amateur fossil hunters and professional paleontologists. Instead of shark teeth, Johnny found the bones of the first baby nodosaur, an armored dinosaur related to the ankylosaurus. Scientists say that this nodosaur died soon after hatching. Later, 19-year-old Cameron Campbell found an adult nodosaur skull in the same area.

And dinosaur discoveries continue to be made. In Arlington, a city between Dallas and Fort Worth, excavations began in 2008 in an area called the Arlington Archosaur Site, located just down the street from a Starbucks. The area, once a swampy bog, holds a treasure trove for scientists. There, researchers have found a complete skeleton of an early duck-billed dinosaur, in addition to a new species of theropod. The area also includes prehistoric crocodiles, fish, sharks, turtles, plants, and trees.

Midland Minnie

LIKE PALEONTOLOGY, the studies of archeology and anthropology are always evolving. New techniques for dating, analyzing, and preserving artifacts continue to be developed. For example, artifacts that include organic matter can now be accurately dated with carbon-14 or radiocarbon dating.

Clay Dough Dino

Plenty of dinosaurs roamed Texas. Do you know which ones? Research which dinosaurs lived in the state—a few are already listed in this chapter. Find out as much as you can about the appearance of one of these dinosaurs, and then make a clay model of it.

Adult supervision required

Materials
★ 2 cups water
★ Food coloring (optional)
★ 3½ cups all-purpose flour
★ ½ cup salt
★ 1 tablespoon cream of tartar
★ 2½ tablespoons vegetable oil
★ Baking sheet or waxed paper

1. Boil the water in a medium-sized pot on the stove.

2. Add food coloring to the water if you want your dinosaur to be a specific color.

3. Mix the dry ingredients—flour, salt, cream of tartar—in a large bowl.

4. Remove the water from the stove.

5. Add the vegetable oil to the water.

6. Pour the water into the large bowl with the dry ingredients. Stir until mixed.

7. Let the clay cool until you can comfortably work with it.

8. Knead the dough on a baking sheet or wax paper.

9. Create your clay dough dinos and let them air dry. If you need to wait until later, store the dough in an airtight container.

Examples of early human life are also being continually discovered. Soon after the Clovis (New Mexico) sites excavated in the 1930s estimated early human life in North America at 10,000 years old, discoveries in Texas forced scientists to take another look.

Midland County is located midway between Fort Worth and El Paso, which is how it got its name. It's located in the Texas High Plains where water is less than plentiful. This area is also called the Permian Basin, an area thick with rocks from the Permian geologic period. The basin is also a significant location for oil and gas, and the petroleum industry has long

Iguanodon skull.

Jim Linwood, Wikimedia Commons

been a chief employer. Oil and gas are fossil fuels that come from the remains of animals and plants from 300 million years ago.

One day in 1953, pipeline welder Keith Glasscock was six miles south of the town of Midland, on the Scharbauer Ranch. He and his son were traipsing around looking for arrowheads; plenty had been found in the Midland area. The son found some bone fragments and brought them to his dad. Glasscock, an amateur archeologist, looked at the area where his son had found the fragments. After looking around more, he found a fossilized skull, a rib, and two bones from a foot—all from a human who lived a very long time ago. This was the first discovery of the Midland Man.

Glasscock didn't disturb the site any further, but notified some archeologists he knew. Four months later, a group of archeologists from Texas and New Mexico arrived. They dug a six-foot-square pit and collected samples of animal life in order to help date the site—extinct species of horses, sloths, mammoths, and four-horned antelope were found. The more searching and analyzing they performed, the more the archeologists became convinced that several early transportation routes had crossed the area.

Other discoveries, such as dinosaur tracks discovered at Fort Stockton, shed more light on the region. Around 100 to 120 million years earlier, 30-foot long iguanodons waded through the shallow waters of the Permian Sea. Trilobite fossils found in the area dated the site to around 360 million years old because that's when the trilobites had died out.

When funding arrived from a New York foundation, the archeologists returned for more extensive excavations of the "Midland Man." More human bones were found. The dry, sandy Midland County had actually once been an oasis with a cool, humid climate that helped preserve fossils.

The bone fragments were sent to the University of Michigan where carbon dating revealed that they were more than 10,000 years old. And that's not all the fragments had to say. The Midland Man was actually "Midland Minnie," an approximately 30-year-old *woman* with bad teeth and type A blood. Hers were the oldest human remains found in the New World so far.

And Midland Minnie wasn't alone. In 2001, US Fish and Wildlife Service workers were digging on the coastal plains south of Houston near the Gulf of Mexico. When they realized they had cut the top off a human skull, they immediately stopped and contacted authorities. While initial indicators suggested it was 13,000 years old, a piece of that skull was sent to the University of Arizona for radiocarbon testing. The skull was determined to be female and 10,700 years old.

Archeological consultant Robert d'Aigle wondered if Brazoria Woman, as this skeleton became known due to her location in Brazoria County, had sunk in the coastal bog or been buried face down. Archeologists from Texas A&M University were called in to help with the excavation. The young woman had been purposefully buried face down with her arms crossing her chest.

Other ancient human remains have been unearthed in Texas as well. Albert Redder and Frank Watt discovered the remains of an adult man and a child in Bosque County on the west bank of the Brazos River in 1970. They were discovered in a rock shelter formed by limestone erosion. The site is known as Horn Shelter 2. Examination of the adult skull places it approximately 11,200 years ago; it's also been determined by scientists from the Smithsonian and various universities that the skeletons did not resemble modern Native Americans. Instead, the discovery from the late Ice Age seemed connected to earlier people, perhaps from the San Patrice and Dalton cultures of the Southeast.

By systematically examining each layer at Horn Shelter 2, scientists have been able to learn more about different groups who have lived and visited the area. Much can be learned about a society by examining what they ate. How did people get their food and prepare it?

Did they share food? What were the social relationships and physical health like?

Life in Texas has been around for a very long time.

The Early Humans of Texas

IF YOU venture into the Lower Pecos area of southwest Texas, look at the rock walls carefully. You just might see a message from someone who lived 4,000 years ago. The canyons and rock shelters along the Pecos, Devils, and Rio Grande Rivers are home to one of the larg-

Pictographs in Seminole Canyon Park.

5 Zereshk, Wikimedia Commons

est collections of prehistoric pictographs in the Americas. While some of the pictographs are found on private land, a large concentration of pictographs is being preserved in Seminole Canyon State Park.

With fibrous plant leaves for brushes and shells or flat rocks for palettes, artists created a significant amount of art. Various minerals provided different hues. Hundreds of pictographs, ranging from a single picture to areas that stretch hundreds of feet, tell the stories of people who lived thousands of years ago.

The purpose and meaning of the rock art aren't always clear. Many of the pictures, referred to as the Pecos River Style art, include spear throwers. It has been suggested that some of the murals show people's beliefs at the time, such as shamanic journeys to the land of the dead. Were the pictographs a means of communication? A historical record? An artist's canvas? We'll never know.

What is known is that life existed long before artists began using the limestone of the Pecos River valley for paintings. Bones of prehistoric mammals—mammoths, camels, ancient bison, giant armadillos, giant short-faced bears—have been uncovered in the Lubbock area. They are dated up to 7,000 years earlier than the paintings.

Midland Minnie and the Horn Shelter Man lived in Texas 10,000 to 12,000 years ago, but what came after them? In the far northeast part of Texas, known as the Panhandle, a hunting and gathering society lived in stone dwellings along the Canadian River. The first excavations at "Old Buried City" done in 1900 uncovered many single room dwellings suggesting a large population.

And then there were the strange arrangements of rocks that west-central Texas ranchers found on their lands. Known as cairns, the circular piles of rocks varied in size, but many looked down on valleys and canyons. Whispers of Indian burial grounds were common, and they were actually correct. When archeologists investigated the stone mounds perched upon ridges above the Brazos and Colorado Rivers, they found the human remains of men, women, and children.

The cairns appeared to be a type of cemetery from the Late Prehistoric time period, from about 800 CE (Common Era) to 1300 CE. During this time, people farmed, picked berries, and hunted both small game and large game, like rabbits and mammoth, in this area of Texas. Spears were the most effective hunting tools.

Water from the Brazos and Colorado Rivers and their tributaries flowed until the year 750, when there was a significant drought. There may have been movement as groups moved to be closer to water or conflict as people

Rock 'n' Art

People have been painting on caves and rocks for a very long time–mostly animals, but various symbols were also common. Were the artists of the rock art trying to communicate something? Many people think so. Try to communicate something by painting a message on a rock.

Materials
★ Rocks
★ Newspaper
★ Old toothbrush
★ Acrylic paints
★ 1- to 2-inch paintbrushes
★ Jar of water

1. Choose a rock or rocks to paint on. Smooth surfaces are usually easier to paint on.

2. Lay out a newspaper to work on.

3. Clean away any excess dirt on the rock with the old toothbrush.

4. Use a different paintbrush with each color or rinse your brush out in the water as needed.

5. Now get creative. Here are some ideas to get you started:

competed for resources. Big game probably died out, and subsequent cultures hunted the smaller bison and deer familiar to us today.

More dirt mounds were found in East Texas, in an area known as Pine Tree Mound. Excavation didn't start until 2004. The artifacts uncovered then point to an important agricultural society, called the Caddo, that existed from the 1300s until possibly the 1700s. Archeologists believe that Pine Tree Mound was the social and political center of the Nadaco Caddo province.

At Pine Tree Mound, 12 to 15 households surrounded three temple mounds and ceremonial buildings where leaders probably lived. Each household was circular, about 20 feet in diameter, and covered in thatch. Not everyone lived in the main village, which probably contained about 125 people. Other homes were scattered in nearby valleys. Ceremony was an important part of the society, and the priests and/or leaders had much power.

The Spanish started arriving by the mid-1500s and traveled a popular trail, the Hasinai Trace, which ran close to Pine Tree Mound. However, little is known about any encounters between the Nadaco Caddo and Europeans. All that is known is that the Nadaco Caddo seemed to fade away. Some may have joined other bands of Caddo. The population may have also been affected by the introduction of disease by the Europeans.

Science has long said that the Clovis society produced the first humans in North America. This theory states that Native Americans first crossed the Bering Land Bridge into North America. Clovis societies were initially identified by the type of type of tools and weapons found at the Clovis site in New Mexico.

Some archeologists question the theory that the first humans in North America were of the Clovis society, ancestors of today's Native Americans. Some studies have produced DNA evidence that says this might not be true. Other archeological sites suggest that human life in the Americas is actually much older. One site is in Chile. Another one may be the Buttermilk Creek site (also known as the Debra L. Friedkin site) in central Texas.

Buttermilk Creek is in Hill Country near the town of Salado. Excavations started in 2006 when archeologist and professor Michael Waters from Texas A&M University excavated tools with smaller blades than those associated with the Clovis culture. Artifacts were discovered in older sediment layers. Waters believes that the over 15,000 artifacts discovered suggest the site is 13.2 to 15.5 thousand years old. There's much disagreement among archeologists, but excavations and analysis continue.

The Texas Missions

By the 16th century, Texas was filled with three types of people.

First, there were the coastal Native Americans, like the Karankawa, who mainly lived off what the ocean provided. Although they were nomadic, the Karankawa remained in a small region, from Galveston Bay southwestward to Corpus Christi Bay. They made their homes on the coast of the long line of barrier islands. Each band of 30 to 40 people was ruled by a chief who let the weather and food supply dictate where they set up their wigwams. Smoke signals between the bands worked as well as today's social media in letting members know where to meet for ceremonies or *mitotes*. At mitotes, the Karankawa enjoyed dancing and playing warlike games. A favorite pastime was wrestling. Occasionally, bands would also join forces to fight off other Native American tribes.

Another group living in Texas was the Plains tribes, such as the Comanche and Apache. Primarily hunters, Plains peoples followed game like the buffalo. They traveled across the Southwest United States and Mexico, often clashing with other tribes on their way.

The last group was the largest—the farmers, known primarily as the Caddo. Made up of many different bands sharing a similar language, the Caddo lived in East and North Texas. Other tribes who spoke a similar language were the smaller groups of Wichita and Pawnee, also found in what is now Texas.

The Caddo people of Texas were divided into two main groups. The Kadohadacho group lived in villages along the Red River near the Texas-Oklahoma border. The other was the Hasinai, who lived in East Texas, Louisiana, Oklahoma, and Arkansas. The Hasinai also lived in large villages. The largest village was located where the city of Nacogdoches now sits.

Many bands made up the Hasinai, a confederacy that called themselves "Tejas" or "those who are friends." Now you know where the state's name came from: it's from the Caddo word *Tejas*.

Caddo land was good land with pine forests and an abundance of water. Pecan and walnut trees provided nuts for eating. Another tree found near the rivers was the bois d'arc, also known as the osage orange tree. Bois d'arc was a strong yet flexible wood used for making bows for hunting and war. The Caddo used stone axes to chop down trees for their weapons or to make the frames of their homes. Long grass and cane covered the tall cone-shaped huts.

Wood was also used to make furniture such as beds and chairs for their homes. Many families had two homes—a winter home and a summer home. The summer home had no walls, only a roof and a floor. But the floor, made of wood or woven cane, allowed air to pass through, keeping the home cooler.

Although primarily farmers, the Caddo did hunt for some food—mainly deer, rabbit, squirrel, and turkey. Sometimes hunting parties set out to hunt buffalo on the plains. The Caddo also picked blackberries, acorns, and persimmons, and dug assorted roots. But their main supply of food was the corn, beans, and squash grown in forest clearings.

The Spanish Land in Texas

ONE DAY in 1528, members of the Karankawa tribe, perhaps a family, walked along the beach of a small island (later called Galveston) about 13 miles long and slightly over a mile wide. Accompanying them were their constant companions—dogs with a distinctly foxlike appearance.

Women wearing skirts of Spanish moss scanned the beach for food. Food was usually gathered from the west side of the island, in the marshy areas between the island and the mainland, but a big storm had come during the night. Perhaps the storm had left behind crab, turtles, or fish for dinner.

The Karankawa people were familiar with the storms that beat down on the coast, covering the barrier islands with water. When the storms came, the Karankawa packed their portable wigwam homes, known as *ba-ak*, into their dugout canoes. Also in the canoes were household items such as baskets and pottery, and bows and arrows for hunting.

Heading inland to escape the storms, the Karankawa could land on the big sandy areas and walk to a safe place or they could take one of the many creeks and rivers heading inland like spiderwebs. After the storms, some Karankawa returned to the islands to see what treasures the storm may have deposited on the beach.

Shouts from the men in the party, dressed in breechcloths of deerskin, demanded the women's attention. The men pointed to a curious

A Texas Thanksgiving

Think Thanksgiving comes from Plymouth Rock? Not according to the people of El Paso. They say that the first thanksgiving celebration was celebrated with Juan de Oñate and his expedition on April 30, 1598. They blazed a trail between Chihuahua City and El Paso, but their journey included many difficulties such as finding enough water and the threat of being captured by Native Americans.

Oñate set off with 500 people, including soldiers and colonists and their families. They marched across the Chihuahuan Desert with 7,000 head of livestock for 50 days. First, they had a week of rain. Then they had intense dry spells. During the last five days, the expedition ran out of food and water. They began eating the desert vegetation. When they reached a river, two people were so frantic to drink that they drowned. Oñate ordered a day of thanksgiving. The feast would include game from the Spaniards and fish from the Native Americans. The meat and fish were roasted over a great bonfire.

Perhaps they made a type of chili with the game, local vegetation, and spices that they may have carried. For your Thanksgiving, you might try this Texas Chili.

Adult supervision required

Texas Chili
- ★ 10 red chile pods (6 ounces canned chopped green chiles will work too)
- ★ ¼ cup cooking oil
- ★ 2 pounds stew meat
- ★ ½ cup chopped onions
- ★ 3 cloves garlic, minced
- ★ 2 teaspoons salt
- ★ 2 teaspoons dried oregano

1. If you are using canned chiles, skip ahead to Step 2. Otherwise, make your own chile paste by washing the chile pods and placing them in a large pan filled with water. Boil over medium heat until soft. Drain most (but not all) of the water. Place the chiles and remaining water into a blender and liquefy.

2. Cook stew meat, onions, and garlic in ½ cup of cooking oil.

3. When the meat is brown, add the chile paste and the remaining ingredients. Simmer, stirring frequently, for 30 minutes.

sight up ahead. A tangle of wood and hides lay on the beach, and among the wreckage were men like they had never seen—men of pale skin, bearded with tangled hair. Although they wore more clothing than the Karankawa, the material was dirty and ripped. Even from a distance, it was easy to see that the creatures were dead or almost so.

The shipwrecked men were explorers from Spain, and while their appearance was the first sighting of Europeans by the Texas Karankawa, the Spanish had seen Native Americans before. These approximately 80 to 90 men were what remained of a Spanish expedition originally headed by Panfilo de Narváez.

The expedition had been plagued with problems from the beginning. Their first ship wrecked in the Caribbean, but the men were able to get a replacement ship in Cuba. They set off for North America, eager to claim some land for Spain. They landed near Tampa Bay, but Narváez and 400 of his men quickly made enemies among the Florida natives when they stole food and made captives of the native people. The native people of Florida fought back. Narváez was captured and never heard from again. The surviving Spaniards realized it was in their best interests to leave Florida.

The remaining Spaniards built three large, crude rafts from nearby trees and the hides of deer and their horses. Horses became a prima-ry food source, with one killed every third day. Metal from saddles and bridles was melted down to make axes and saws. Any spare clothing was put to work as a sail. With each of the rafts carrying about 50 men and their remaining belongings, the rafts sat low in the Gulf waters; it was unlikely they would stay afloat in the open sea. They hoped to reach a Spanish settlement, Santisteban del Puerto, in Mexico.

Álvar Núñez Cabeza de Vaca was now leader of the expedition. The raft carrying Cabeza de Vaca entered a fierce storm at the Río del Espíritu Santo—the Mississippi River—and strong winds and waves separated the rafts. The men clung to their rafts as huge waves tossed them about.

The Karankawa before him looked little like the angry native people he had left behind in Florida. These people had painted bodies and pieces of cane in their lips and nipples. Some were dirtier than he and his men, wearing what looked like mud. Had Cabeza de Vaca examined them more closely, he would have noticed that mosquitoes avoided those painted with mud, which was really a mixture of dirt and shark or alligator grease. His name for the rescuers was the Quevene Indians, although later accounts suggest they may have been the Cujane band of the Karankawan group.

On the morning after the shipwreck, Cabeza de Vaca realized that the small group that had originally found him had been replaced by about a hundred with bows and arrows. According to Cabeza de Vaca, "we could not defend ourselves, as there were scarcely three of us who could stand on their feet.... They came, and we tried to quiet them the best we could and save ourselves, giving them beads and bells. Each one of them gave me an arrow in token of friendship, and by signs they gave us to understand that on the following morning they would come back with food, as then they had none."

The Karankawa brought the survivors fish and roots to dine on, as well as fresh water. Stronger, the Spaniards tried to take off again, but they didn't get very far before huge waves sank what was left of their raft and drowned three more men. The remaining men swam back to shore, but were freezing. It was winter. The Karankawa who had been providing food took them to their village and put them in a hut with fires to warm them. Once the Spaniards recovered, they were expected to work, just as everyone in the village did.

The winter was hard as sickness of the stomach spread among Spaniards and Karankawa alike. By the next spring, half the Karankawa had died and only 13 Spaniards and an African slave still lived. Cabeza de Vaca named the island Malhado or Isle of Misfortune. The Karankawa blamed the Spaniards and threatened to kill them, but for some reason did not.

Álvar Núñez Cabeza de Vaca.
Billy Hathorn, Wikimedia Commons

The Spaniards were able to move inland, where they stayed with another south Texas tribe, the Coahuiltecans. When it warmed, 10 of the Spaniards traveled south along the coast to Mexico. Cabeza de Vaca remained in the eastern Texas wilderness with the Moroccan, Estevanico, and two other Spaniards. Cabeza de Vaca learned to survive by trading and practicing medicine. He may have been the first European merchant in Texas. He carried seashells inland and traded them for red ochre and bison skins, which he took back to the coast and traded for food. He developed a reputation as a healer among the native people.

Eventually, the shipwrecked Spaniards made the decision to leave. They met another tribe, the Quevenes, who spoke of three Christians like them. The Quevenes took Cabeza de Vaca and his men to the others. They were three Spaniards from the shipwreck. This group of seven were all that was left of an expedition that began with 400.

The surviving Spaniards were intent on finding a Spanish colony. They struck out in a southwesterly direction, traveling barefoot for 2,400 miles. It took a few years, but they finally met up with another Spanish expedition. They eventually made it to Mexico City in July 1536, eight years after their shipwreck on the Isle of Misfortune.

New Spain

IN 1519, the Spanish governor of Jamaica sent an expedition to explore the land bordering the Gulf of Mexico, which is now Texas and the southern United States. Surely there was more to this new land than these locations, perhaps a shortcut to Asia. Alonso Álvarez de Pineda set out with four ships and 270 men to explore the Gulf of Mexico. He started at Florida's western coast and made the discovery that Florida was not an island, as previously thought, but a peninsula. For weeks, they sailed farther along the Gulf Coast and were impressed when they came upon the Mississippi River. Álvarez de Pineda noted the many barrier islands of Texas and included them in the first map of the Gulf of Mexico. The Spanish began to realize that they were looking at a vast land, much larger than Spain.

The Spaniards had a new goal in the New World. They were searching for the fabled seven cities of Cibola, cities of great wealth. The fact that other Spanish explorers had secured the riches of the Incas in Peru and the

★ Álvar Núñez Cabeza de Vaca, the First Known European in Texas

Álvar Núñez Cabeza de Vaca was born into Spanish nobility around 1490 but was orphaned as a teenager. He chose a military life and left Spain in 1527 on the royal expedition that landed him in Texas.

The Native Americans of Texas impressed Cabeza de Vaca, so their mistreatment at the hands of the Spanish upset him. When he returned to Spain, he wrote about his eight-year adventure in the New World.

Cabeza de Vaca returned to the Americas and served as a territorial governor in Paraguay. His fairness to the natives bothered some of the colonists, who accused him of corruption. Cabeza de Vaca was sent back to Spain, convicted, and banished from the Americas. He was pardoned when he was in his 60s and allowed to serve as a judge in Seville until his death.

Aztec in Mexico made the idea of another wealthy empire easy to believe. Expeditions set out in search of Cibola.

None of the explorers was more ambitious nor extensive in searching than Francisco Vázquez de Coronado. Setting out four years after Cabeza de Vaca's return to Spanish society, Coronado's search extended from California to Kansas to Texas. At Palo Duro Canyon, second in size only to the Grand Canyon, the expedition met with a violent storm. Hail rained down on their conquistador helmets. He and his men killed or ran off any Native American tribes that resisted their efforts, but the expedition was in vain. Cibola was never found.

Palo Duro Canyon. Leaflet, Wikimedia Commons

The French Arrive

By the late 1600s, the Spanish had some competition from the French, who had already explored Louisiana to the east. The French explorers, led by René-Robert Cavelier, sieur de La Salle, were intent upon establishing a French colony in the Gulf region. La Salle had already explored the Mississippi River region and claimed the area for France, naming it Louisiana.

La Salle set off from France with almost 300 people on four ships, yet only 180 landed at Matagorda Bay in Texas. They decided to build their settlement, Fort St. Louis, three miles inland on the banks of Garcitas Creek. Food and shelter were the first items of importance. According to fort commander Henri Joutel, the area had plenty of reeds, but little wood. So hunting parties had two purposes when they set out—killing animals for food and bringing back wood for building. The grueling work in establishing a community in the wilderness coupled with disease and exposure led to the deaths of half the colonists within the first six months. According to Joutel, the remaining colonists had two problems: boredom and the Karankawa. After some of the colonists stole canoes from the Karankawa, relationships worsened. A group led by La Salle and Joutel left to continue exploration. It was La Salle's last expedition. He was ambushed, possibly by a disgruntled follower. Joutel led another group of settlers to Canada before returning to France.

The remaining colonists did not know what had happened to their leaders. But it's believed that in the spirit of Christmas in 1688 or 1689, they invited the Karankawa to join the festivities.

When the Spanish finally discovered the location of Fort St. Louis, all that remained were ruins. It wasn't until later that the story of the empty settlement was explained by children who survived. One couple in the expedition, the Talons, had six small children when they settled in Texas. Five of the six children were found living with area tribes years later. Two sons were found with the Hasinai. Two other sons and a daughter were with the Karankawa. The children grew up as members of these Native American societies. The youngest two boys even forgot how to speak French. One of the children, Jean-Baptíste Talon, reported that the Karankawa killed everyone else around Christmas time in 1688.

The Missions

As THE conquistadors failed to uncover any cities of gold, they concentrated on settlement. Other European countries were interested in the same land. Spain knew that the best way to claim the land was to settle it with Spanish citizens and to convert native people to Christians loyal to Spain. Catholic priests began accompanying explorers by 1543.

Unlike other Spanish expeditions that began at the coast and moved west, a special order of the Catholic Church, the Franciscan missionaries, began in New Mexico and spread east to Texas. In the beginning, efforts were concentrated in West Texas, but a series of disasters, including the Great Pueblo Revolt in New Mexico, had the Franciscans looking at South and East Texas. The Franciscans built the first mission in Texas in 1632. It was unsuccessful and soon closed. It would be more than 50 years before widespread missions were built.

San Juan Bautista was one of the more successful missions. Established south of the Rio Grande in 1699, it became a gateway for Franciscans establishing missions throughout Texas.

The Texas missions were intended to be homes for area natives, who would learn about Christianity, agriculture, and crafts. Missions were largely self-sufficient complexes that usually started with the building of a church, and then the clearing of the land. Crops were planted. Crafts were another part of the industry, whether it was weaving or making pottery. Missionaries often attracted followers by offering small gifts. Native Americans may also have

Build an Aqueduct

The missions in the San Antonio area constructed aqueducts for irrigating their crops. Aqueducts can actually be used to move water for any purpose. The invention originally came from the Roman Empire.

Materials
★ Plywood base
★ Flower foam cubes found at florists or craft stores
★ Level
★ Butter knife
★ Paint or pottery clay (optional)

Aqueduct in San Antonio, Bexar County, Texas. Library of Congress (HABS TEX,15-SANT.V,4—4)

1. Decide on the general design of your aqueduct. For ideas, look at www.pbs.org/wgbh/nova/lostempires /roman/aqueduct.html

2. Cut a number of floral foam cubes, each slightly shorter than the previous, and line them up on a plywood base.

3. Place a level on top of the cubes to see if they angle downward, just slightly, so that water can run along your "aqueduct."

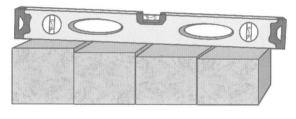

4. One by one, remove each block, carve an arch into the base with a butter knife, and replace it in the line.

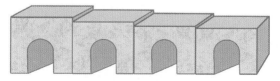

5. When all the arches are carved, glue the blocks to the base.

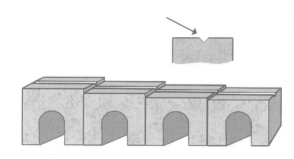

6. After the glue has dried, carve a trough into the top surface of the aqueduct.

7. Because the blocks are porous, you will not be able to run water through the trough unless you seal it. Either paint it or cover it completely in modeling clay. Once dry, you can run water from the high end to the low end.

Mission Concepción. Karen Bush Gibson

been most attracted by the protection against the fierce Comanche and Apache or the food available in the winter months. In some situations, the Native Americans were then captured and treated as slaves.

The mission bells structured the day. Morning bells rang to wake people and call them to mass. After breakfast, the Native Americans worked in the fields or the workshop. When the bell rang at noon, everyone knew it was mealtime. A typical meal was corn, vegetables, and fruit. On Sundays, beef was served. Evening bells meant evening services and dinner.

Missions had the greatest success in a concentrated area near the rivers of Hill Country. The first in that area was Mission Concepción. It first opened its doors in 1716, but it wasn't until it moved near the San Antonio River that it began to thrive. Four other missions were established in the area on either side of the river. Canals were built to use the San Antonio River for irrigation.

A presidio or town sprang up around the missions—San Antonio de Bexar. It became a center of commerce in addition to a crossroads in the New Spain frontier. It also became home to a military garrison. San Antonio soon became the most importance place in Texas.

By the end of the 18th century, the mission populations in Texas had dropped but so had the population of many of the Native American tribes. They experienced increased mortality primarily due to the introduction of diseases from the Europeans—smallpox, measles, and typhoid. The population of the Caddo confederation suffered greatly. Other tribes, such as the Karankawa, totally disappeared.

Mexican Independence

DURING THE colonial era, European countries often competed for the best colonies. Sometimes these struggles led to war. Spain and France battled during the Napoleonic wars. Putting resources toward battles interrupted trade ventures that the countries relied on for income. Like other empires, Spain decided to place its financial burden on its colonies through taxation and by calling in loans and mortgages. When this didn't raise enough money, Spanish officials took everything of value from the colonial churches.

The main income from Texas came from agriculture and ranching, yet raiders from native tribes could wipe out a successful harvest or steal livestock. Rounding up the large number of wild horses, or mustangs, was a potentially

The most elaborate of the Texas missions were made of stone and lime mortar with ornate frescoes around the thick doorways.
Karen Bush Gibson

profitable enterprise for horse trading. Yet Plains tribes like the Comanche highly valued horses and anyone with horses was a potential target.

Beans, chiles, refined cane sugar, cotton, and wheat were grown commercially. Enough corn was also produced to feed settlers and military units. Overworking the land and droughts adversely affected farms and cattle ranches. And the environment was harsh as well. Only San Antonio had any type of irrigation system and that irrigation system fell into disrepair as the populations of the missions decreased.

The Mexican territory known as New Spain, which included most of Texas, had grown in the approximately 300 years that Spain had occupied it. Intermarriage between the Spanish and Mexico's native people resulted in a new class of people that went by many names— mixed bloods, mestizos, Mexicans. Like the people of the American colonies 40 years earlier, the Mexican people were feeling restrained. A need for independence was stirring in the air.

Father Miguel Hidalgo y Costilla, a parish priest in a small agricultural town, mobilized forces to fight against the Spanish in September 1810. For several years, skirmishes between the Spanish loyal to Spain and the Mexicans intent on independence occurred. And for awhile, Mexicans seems to be gaining ground against the Spanish.

Some of these battles took place in the Texas province, and on January 22, 1811, the rebels unseated the governor, Manuel de Salcedo. Although part of the Spanish colony, Texas wasn't as settled as parts of Mexico due to the constant threats from the fierce Comanche and Apache raiders.

But Spain had competition for Texas: the United States. The newly expanding United States had bought the Louisiana Territory from the French for $15 million in 1803. The Louisiana Territory was just to the east and north of Texas and in fact included some of the farthest northern sections of present-day Texas, including the Panhandle. There was talk that perhaps the southern border of the United States should be the Rio Grande instead of the Red River.

Some Americans decided it was their right to go where they wanted. And they wanted to relocate from the former Louisiana Territory to Texas. They were joined by traders, outlaws, and even US soldiers. Slipping past borders into Texas was nothing new, and Americans explored Texas, rode with the Comanche, and hunted buffalo on the plains.

When Spain and the United States signed the Adams-Onis Treaty in 1819, which gave Florida to the United States and Texas to Spain, these new Texas transplants were angry. Three hundred people left Natchez, Mississippi, for what they called the "Republic of Texas." Led

Father Miguel Hidalgo y Costilla.

Library of Congress (LC-USZ62-98851)

by merchant James Long, these Americans declared Texas independence in 1819. Spanish forces drove most of the 300 Americans back into Louisiana. They captured James Long and imprisoned him in Mexico, where he was killed six months later by a guard.

After a string of successful battles, Spain resumed control over much of Mexico. Only in Texas did the rebels occasionally find success. That is, until the 1813 Battle of Medina (also known as the Gutierrez-Magee Expedition), in what the Texas State Historical Association calls "the bloodiest action ever fought on Texas soil." Twenty miles south of San Antonio on a battleground in an oak grove called Medina, 1,400 republican rebels who disagreed with the ruling of a monarchy fought against the Spanish royalists led by General Joaquín de Arredondo. One of his young officers was a Lieutenant Antonio López de Santa Anna.

The rebels were ambushed by the royalist army. During a four-hour siege, all but a hundred of the rebels were slaughtered. The Spanish army lost only 55 men. When the battle ended, those 55 were buried, while the dead bodies of approximately 1,300 rebels were left on the battlefield.

The leaders of the independence movement, including Father Hidalgo, were executed by firing squad. It seemed that Mexico's independence would just be a dream until another priest, José María Morelos y Pavón, led the quest for Mexican independence. Mexico declared their independence and drafted a constitution. Although some battles took place in southern Texas, Texas mainly watched to see what would happen and how it would affect the Texas region.

Although Spanish rule continued, rebellion against the Spanish crown continued to grow in the New World. Dissatisfaction with Spain's ruler Ferdinand VII, who insisted on absolute power over the colonies, also grew. When Napoleon overthrew Spain, the South American colonies declared their independence.

On July 21, 1821, the Spanish flag was finally lowered from San Antonio. New Spain was now Mexico. The first governor of Texas in the new country of Mexico had soldiers collect for burial the bones of the soldiers who had died at the Battle of Medina. After nine years, the men who had fought for Mexican independence on Texas soil were given an honorable burial under an oak tree on the Medina battlefield.

The Republic of Texas Is Born

Although the Mexican War of Independence had ended, the influence of Spain remained. Spain had introduced horses, livestock, guns, Christianity, ranching, farming, and the Spanish language.

The new Mexican government made Coahuila and Texas one state—Coahuila y Tejas, although many Tejanos and colonists saw Texas as separate. Coahuila y Tejas was the northernmost state in Mexico with a western border shared with the Nuevo Mexico territory and a northern and eastern border with the United States. Although one of the largest Mexican states in land size, it was not large in population. Due to its proximity to the United States, the Mexican government wanted the state populated. Settlers could buy land for two cents an acre as long as they became Mexican citizens and converted to Catholicism.

The population of settlements in Texas began to increase. Laredo, a city just to the north of the Rio Grande, had managed to double in size due to colonists known as Tejanos, people of Spanish, Mexican, and Indian blood. All Tejanos called Tejas or Texas home; some were even born there. Tejanos built churches, ranchos, and towns.

The largest of the Texas settlements was also the oldest, San Antonio de Béxar. When Mexico first obtained independence, the population of San Antonio was approximately 2,000, mainly people who had relocated from Coahuila and Nuevo León. There was also a group of settlers from the Canary Islands, a Spanish province off the coast of Africa.

The American Colony

PERHAPS THE largest number of settlers in Texas came from the United States. Knowing that the United States still had its eye on Texas forced the new Mexican government to take more control over the settlement of Texas.

Many Americans were interested in moving to Texas after reading about it in newspapers. They could get land cheaply, just $1.25 an acre. One man in particular was Moses Austin, a leader in the American lead industry. When the Bank of St. Louis failed, the Austin family lost their fortune, and Moses was looking for a new venture.

In late 1820, before Mexican independence, Austin visited San Antonio to request permission to establish a colony of 300 families. Although he was refused at his first meeting with Governor Antonio María Martínez, he was successful the second time when he returned with a Dutch businessman and resident of San Antonio, Baron de Bastrop. Bastrop and Austin were old acquaintances and Bastrop was a favorite of the Spanish government. Governor Martínez reconsidered and granted Austin's petition.

On his return home, Moses Austin became ill from pneumonia, but he was obsessed with seeing his plan for the Texas colony succeed. He lived for two more months. On his deathbed, he pleaded with his son, Stephen, to finish what he had started.

Stephen Fuller Austin was a businessman, politician, and lawyer. After receiving permission from the Spanish government to continue his father's work, Stephen Austin chose an area along the Brazos and Colorado Rivers. He promoted the Anglo-American colony. But when Mexico won its war against Spain, Austin had to travel to Mexico City to renegotiate the agreement.

The younger Austin acted as the land contractor between the colonists and the Mexican government in what was called the empresario system. He would arrange for the head of a household to receive 640 acres. If the head of household had family, his wife and children would bring him an additional 320 acres each. For each slave he owned, the head of the household would receive an extra 80 acres. As empresario, Austin would receive 67,000 acres for his services in each contract. He was given three contracts in all, each for settling 300 families.

Austin mapped and surveyed the territory and made arrangements for the land allotments. He was the liaison between the colonists and the Mexican government. Although the colonists would come from the United States, the colony had to function as a part of Mexico. As colonists began arriving in late 1821, it was Austin's job to make certain they behaved. Although Austin was in charge, he allowed the colonists to form a militia, courts, and a local government. He encouraged trade by establishing ports.

After the Anglo colony was settled, Mexico passed a colonization law in 1824 that set up regulations for further colonization, including the right to refuse immigrants if national security was at stake. When government officials toured the colonies, the found that Mexican influence was being lost in places, particularly east of San Antonio. Mexican president Anastasio Bustamente refused to allow any more Americans to immigrate into Texas. The Mexican government also outlawed slavery and began collecting customs duties or taxes on imports and exports.

The Anglo-American colonists and Tejanos were furious. When settlers in Nacogdoches refused to surrender their guns to the Mexican battalion, a battle began. Settlers formed their own militia and sent messengers to other settlements asking for help. And help came. James Bullock was elected as leader of the Texas colonists, and he and his militia captured the Old Stone Fort and took control of Nacogdoches.

Mexico sent additional troops to Texas and continued to insist that taxes and trade duties be paid. Authorities refused to allow ships to dock in Galveston Bay until they made a 140-mile trip to pay duties on cargo. Many ship captains refused and more gunfire was exchanged with the garrison located at Anahuac.

Mexican authorities reinforced their numbers with runaway slaves from Louisiana. William Barret Travis and Patrick Jack arrived to retrieve the escaped slaves in Anahuac on Galveston Bay. Instead, the two lawyers were arrested and held without trial at the garrison

Stephen Austin.

at Anahuac. More than 150 Texans captured the garrison and the cavalry station there. They agreed to trade the captured soldiers for Travis and Jack, but at the last minute, the officer in charge, Colonel Juan Davis Bradburn, refused to release the prisoners.

The conflict between the groups turned into a battle. The Texans supported politicians known as Federalists because the Federalists supported democracy with more freedom for the states and regions. The Federalists supported Mexico's Constitution of 1824. Based on both the Spanish and American constitutions, the Constitution of 1824 made Catholicism the official religion and made it eligible for financial support from the government. The president and vice president, elected by the legislative bodies of the states, served four years. There were limitations to the leaders' power.

However, the Centralists were in power in the capital, Mexico City. They wanted a stronger central government that made all the decisions. This was similar to the government in Spain, where the king made all the decisions. When the Centralists took over the Mexican government in late 1829, they stopped immigration from the United States. They also increased the military presence in Texas.

The leader of the Federalists was Antonio López de Santa Anna, who would later refer to himself as the "Napoleon of the West" and be considered enemy number one for the Texans. For now, Texans wanted Texas to be a separate state. They asked for exemptions from custom duties for three years and wanted the ban on US immigration lifted.

By the beginning of 1833, Santa Anna's men had overthrown the government in Mexico City and he had declared himself president of a new government. In slightly over two years, Santa Anna abolished the constitution and state governments. He became a dictator, suppressing revolts in any way he could.

Both colonists and Tejanos became increasingly uneasy with Santa Anna, who actually supported the Centralist government, not the Federalist one he had fought for. He abolished the 1824 Constitution in addition to the government in Coahuila and Texas. Speculation began to spread about what would happen if anyone defied him. Santa Anna's army was given free rein to attack, loot, and commit rape in any towns that expressed opposition.

The situation between the Anglos and the Mexican government continued to deteriorate. Small groups tried to secede from Mexico without success. Settlers begin talking about creating a new country, the Republic of Texas.

Stephen Austin wasn't certain this was the right move. Austin had long been the voice of reason, believing that things could be worked out between the colonists and the Mexican

General D. Antonio López de Santa Anna, president of the Republic of Mexico.

government. But he took his job of representing the people of Texas seriously. He presented a petition to the Mexican government to recognize Texas as an independent state and allow immigration from the United States to resume. Before a decision could be made, the people of Mexico City were hit with a cholera epidemic. Austin himself almost died from it.

Austin made plans to return to Texas. He made one last attempt with the Mexican government in a letter. His letter ended with the closing, "God and Texas." Austin was promptly arrested and held in a Mexico City jail for 28 months. Formal charges were never filed, but informally it was said that he was inciting rebellion in Texas.

After his imprisonment, Austin became one of the leaders in the independence movement. He traveled throughout the United States, drumming up public support for Texas. In Washington, he unsuccessfully appealed for military support and the annexation of Texas by the United States.

Texas Fights for Independence

SANTA ANNA sent General Martín Perfecto de Cos, his brother-in-law, to arrest Texas troublemakers and seize arms. The Texans refused to surrender anything, starting with the cannon of the town of Gonzales.

Gonzales owned a bronze cannon that was little more than a noisemaker. During the Mexican War of Independence, the Spanish had blocked the ignition with a metal spike. For four years, Gonzales had used the cannon to alert residents to threats from the Comanche, and now the Mexican army wanted the cannon. The colonists refused, burying the cannon in a peach orchard west of town.

Lieutenant Francisco Castañeda arrived at Gonzales on September 29, 1835, with over a hundred men to seize the cannon and arrest all who resisted. They camped west of the Guadalupe River and sent word requesting a meeting with the town alcalde, or mayor. Casteñada was told that the mayor was unavailable.

When the Mexican troops arrived at the Guadalupe River the next day, all rafts and boats used for crossing the river had been moved to the east bank. Hidden in the trees and bushes were armed colonists, the "Original Old Gonzales 18." That number soon increased to 150, while a plea went out to neighboring towns for aid.

Meanwhile, the Mexican forces moved upriver in search of a better location to cross. Colonists worried not only that the Mexican army would succeed, but also that they would be joined by additional forces. They decided to take the offensive. Digging up the Gonzales cannon, they attempted to make it functional.

They removed the metal spike and began loading the barrel with scrap metal and gunpowder.

On the evening of October 1, about 50 armed colonists took the cannon and crossed the river in the middle of the night, but the fog made it impossible to see anything in the moonlight. By morning, when the fog cleared, shots were fired in earnest, leading to one casualty among the Mexican soldiers.

The cannon the people of Gonzales sought to defend was fired. A huge boom sounded, but the cannon caused no damage. Still, it was the "Texas shot heard round the world" and signaled the beginning of the Texas Revolution on October 2, 1835.

The incident at Gonzales proved to be the catalyst. The Texas Republican Army formed with Stephen F. Austin as its commander. They marched to defend San Antonio de Bexar in late October 1835. There they confronted Santa Anna's Centralista forces in the first Battle of Béxar, the first major battle of the Texas Revolution. A grueling five-day battle resulted in the 600-man Texas army winning and driving out forces led by Mexican General Martín Perfecto de Cos. While most of the Texas soldiers returned home, a small group remained at the Alamo.

The Goliad Massacre occurred soon afterward. Santa Anna declared that according to Mexican law foreigners who engaged in battle against Mexico were pirates, who would be executed. He then proceeded to order that over 300 Texas soldiers being held as prisoners be killed.

The Alamo

MISSION SAN Francisco de Solano was established on the Rio Grande in 1700. Founded by Father Antonio de San Buenaventura y Olivares, its purpose was to convert the Coahuiltecan people to Catholicism and the Spanish way of life. Father Olivares visited Texas in 1709 and was impressed with San Antonio. When the population of Mission Solano began to drop, he suggested to the Spanish viceroy, Marques de Valero, that the mission be moved to San Antonio.

The viceroy gave permission, and the mission was rechristened in San Antonio as San Antonio de Valero. Mission San Antonio de Valero served as a home to missionaries and Native American converts for almost 70 years. In 1745, a hundred Coahuiltecan from the mission rushed to the aid of the people of nearby San Fernando when they were attacked by Apache.

In 1793, Mission San Antonio de Valero passed to the control of local authorities. Its church, never completed, and the adobe houses and buildings were reborn as a military garrison known as the Alamo. It was there that the greatest battle of the Texas Revolution would take place in early 1836.

Tejanos, colonists, and Americans joined together. Approximately 200 men were ready to fight, ranging from 16 to 56 years of age. Few were soldiers. Instead, they were farmers and colonists, doctors and lawyers. There were also women and children inside the Alamo.

Some defenders came with well-known reputations. One was Jim Bowie, an American frontiersman known for his fighting skills and the hunting knife that had been named after him. Also present was Davy Crockett. After serving Tennessee for a time in the US legislature, Crockett had returned to what he loved most, the frontier. And the frontier was now Texas.

Bowie shared leadership at the Alamo with William Barret Travis, a lawyer who had moved to Texas as a colonist at age 22. But Bowie fell ill, and soon Travis assumed command. When President Santa Anna arrived with the Mexican army on February 23, 1836, Travis could see that they were hopelessly outnumbered. He sent messengers to Sam Houston and other leaders in the Texas independence movement. They needed help at the Alamo. The most famous of his letters was addressed "To the People of Texas and all Americans in the World."

I am besieged, by a thousand or more of the Mexicans under Santa Anna. I have sustained a continual Bombardment & cannonade for 24 hours & have not lost a man.

Mission San Antonio de Valero.
Library of Congress (HABS TEX,15-SANT,15—18)

Colonel Davy Crockett. Library of Congress (LC-DIG-pga-04179)

The enemy has demanded a surrender at discretion, otherwise, the garrison are to be put to the sword, if the fort is taken. I have answered the demand with a cannon shot, & our flag still waves proudly from the walls. I shall never surrender or retreat. Then, I call on you in the name of Liberty, of patriotism & everything dear to the American character, to come to our aid, with all dispatch. The enemy is receiving reinforcements daily & will no doubt increase to three or four thousand in four or five days. If this call is neglected, I am determined to sustain myself as long as possible & die like a soldier who never forgets what is due to his own honor & that of his country. Victory or Death.

A 13-day siege commenced at the Alamo. Santa Anna's troops moved in from the southwest. On the fourth day, a cold front brought dropping temperatures and rain. Still, the people of the Alamo could detect the blue uniforms of the Mexican forces. While the people of the Alamo subsisted on their dwindling provisions, Santa Anna took what he needed from ranches surrounding the city.

While the Alamo's forces defended themselves against pounding artillery, Santa Anna sent spare troops to intercept reinforcements coming to the Alamo. Two days later, Santa Anna's reinforcements numbered 1,100. Santa Anna considered the men at the Alamo traitors. They would be given no quarter, no mercy.

Unknown to the people at the Alamo, the provisional Texas government at Washington-on-the-Brazos was moving ahead. An election held February 1, 1836, chose 44 delegates from Texas towns and settlements. The delegates and other interested leaders met at Washington-on-the-Brazos a month later. Of the delegates, two were born in Texas, one in Mexico, and the rest were Americans.

Soon after the writing of the Constitution of the Republic of Texas, word came that Santa Anna's army was headed to Washington-on-the-Brazos. The newborn Texas government evacuated to Hattiesburg.

George C. Childress presented a resolution for independence from Mexico. Based on the US Declaration of Independence, the delegates unanimously adopted the Texas Declaration of Independence and 50 men signed it. The Republic of Texas was born on March 2, 1836.

Men ages 17 to 50 were expected to give military service to the Republic of Texas. In return for service, they would receive land bounties. Those who refused would forfeit lands and citizenship in Texas. Sam Houston was appointed the commander in chief of the army. He immediately left the convention and got to work. Government officials drafted the Constitution of the Republic of Texas, also based on the US

Constitution. There would be executive, legislative, and judicial branches. The president could serve one two-year term, and could not succeed himself. Senators would serve three-year terms, and congressmen one.

Back at the Alamo, the people grimly noted the red flag raised by Mexican forces. Knowing the impossible odds for success, Travis allowed anyone who wanted to leave the Alamo to do so. Only one man left. As the troops prepared for the last battle, Travis put his most precious possession on a piece of twine and around the neck of 15-month-old Angelina Dickinson. It was a gold ring set with a banded agate, known as cat's-eye. It had been given to Travis by a woman he hoped to marry. The ring survived the battle and today is on display at the Alamo, the most visited site in all of Texas.

Before dawn could settle over the Alamo on March 6, Santa Anna gave the order to attack. Defenders rushed to the wall and fired into the dark. Travis died defending the north wall where Mexican troops were pouring in. The men of the Alamo fought against impossible odds, waiting for help that never came. The Alamo fell to Santa Anna in its final 90-minute battle.

The Battle of the Alamo became legendary, with numerous stories circulating among the Texan colonists. Some were true, some were not, and some no one knows for certain. What

Build a Replica of the Alamo

The Alamo is the most important building in the history of Texas. Originally a mission, it later served as a military installation in San Antonio. The Alamo was not just one building, but a 4.2-acre complex that included a church and long barrack. Today, the complex also includes a museum, gift shop, and library. Construction had not been completed on the walls and roof of the church. The long barrack was the quarters for the Spanish missionaries, and during the Battle of the Alamo was where the Texans made their last stand.

In this activity, you will make a model of the Alamo.

Materials
★ 6 pounds of modeling clay
★ Flat piece of cardboard
★ Butter knife

Study the map of the Alamo. Use two-thirds of your clay for the long barracks, and the remaining clay on the church. Mold the clay into the shape desired, using the butter knife to smooth the edge. Place your building models on the cardboard that will serve as your base.

You can use small toy people and/or objects for the inside of the Alamo.

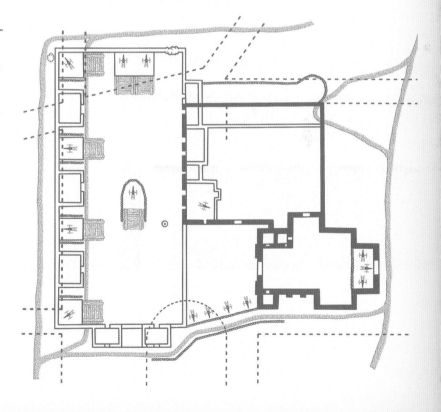

Battle of the Alamo, Percy Moran.

is known is that while all the white men defending the Alamo died, almost twenty people survived. The women and children who were spared were the families of the dead soldiers.

The survivors of the Alamo were allowed to leave. Some, like Susanna Dickinson and her daughter, Angelina, went to Sam Houston's camp to report what had happened before returning home.

An African American slave named Joe, who served Travis and participated in the battle, also survived. He was believed to be in his 20s, although his exact age was unknown. Joe stayed with Houston's troops until the end of the war. Then he was returned to the Travis family in South Carolina. When the one-year anniversary of the Battle of San Jacinto came, Joe disappeared. The Travis family considered him a runaway slave. They put a notice in the Telegraph and Texas Register, offering $50 for his return. Joe reportedly returned to Texas and was last seen in Austin in 1875.

News reached the convention that the Alamo had fallen and that Mexican armies were moving east. The Texas constitution was signed at midnight on March 16. David G. Burnet was elected president by the delegates, and Lorenzo de Zavala vice-president.

Santa Anna called the battle a "small affair" and continued conquering Texas settlements. Sam Houston watched Santa Anna's movements. When Mexican forces split, Houston and his 900 men advanced to San Jacinto along Buffalo Bayou.

General Houston assembled his troops at 3:30 in the afternoon. Many Mexican soldiers were enjoying an afternoon fiesta, perhaps not worried by the bearded ragtag group of Texas rebels, of which only about 50 even owned uniforms.

Cries of "Remember the Alamo!" filled the air as the Texans attacked the Mexican army in an 18-minute battle for the independence of Texas. Two small cannons broke down barricades as 910 men fired their guns. When the guns were empty, they used their rifles as clubs and pulled out their knives. They fought hand-to-hand combat, never letting up.

Mexico lost 630 soldiers in the Battle of San Jacinto while the remaining 730 were taken prisoner. Only nine Texans lost their lives. Thirty-four were injured, include Sam Houston.

Santa Anna's body could not be found. Houston ordered a search of the area, and the next day they discovered Santa Anna hiding in the grass, dressed as a foot soldier. Santa Anna was brought to Houston. Santa Anna believed the capture of the Napoleon of the West was such a great honor for Houston that he should show Santa Anna mercy. Houston, recovering from a gunshot wound to the ankle, disagreed.

"What claim have you to mercy when you showed none at the Alamo or at Goliad?" Houston countered. After talking for nearly two hours, Santa Anna agreed to order all Mexican troops to leave Texas.

The new officials of the Republic of Texas met with the prisoner Santa Anna on May 14, 1836, to sign the treaty ending the revolution. They met at Velasco, one of the earliest capitals of the Republic of Texas. Velasco was a port city on the Brazos River a few miles from the Gulf of Mexico.

There were actually two treaties. The main treaty, the Treaty of Velasco, called for the end

 ## The Floating Capitol

A steamboat called the *Cayuga* had been active during the revolution, carrying supplies and people where needed. When Santa Anna's troops advanced upon the unofficial government in Hattiesburg, the *Cayuga* spirited officials away and for two weeks was the floating capital of Texas.

of the hostilities and the release of prisoners. It also set the Rio Grande as the boundary between Mexico and Texas. A second, secret treaty allowed for the release of Santa Anna at Veracruz so that he could work with the Mexican government in adopting the treaty and recognizing Texas's independence.

Although many in Texas were calling for Santa Anna's execution, Santa Anna did as promised. However, the Mexican legislature refused to adopt the treaty or recognize the independence of Texas. According to Mexico, Texas wasn't independent until the Mexican War.

The Republic of Texas

Texans began the task of building their new country, the Republic of Texas. While a majority of Texans wanted to be admitted to the United States, President Andrew Jackson, and later Martin Van Buren, refused due to ongoing tensions with Mexico.

Eleven days before the first presidential election for the Republic of Texas, Sam Houston agreed to run. He overwhelmingly defeated his opponents, Henry Smith and Stephen Austin. Austin served briefly as secretary of state but he died soon after his appointment, at the age of 43. His contribution to the settlement of Texas, however, won him the title of father of Texas.

A redesigned Lone Star flag for the Republic was raised in January 1839. Red and white stripes of equal width ran across the flag, while a blue background covered the upper left corner. On the blue field was a five-pointed white star.

The First Governor

SAM HOUSTON, the youngest child in his family, grew up on a Virginia plantation until the death of his father. The family then moved to a farm in eastern Tennessee. Sam resisted working on the family farm or in his brothers' store, and ran away at age 16 to live with the Cherokee people on the other side of the Tennessee River. He lived with and was adopted by Chief Oolooteka. Sam was given the Cherokee name Colonneh, or "the Raven." His experience led to a lifelong friendship with the Cherokee and empathy with Native Americans.

Houston later became a soldier, fighting with Andrew Jackson's troops. His natural military strategy led to promotions and recognition. He left the military to study and practice law for a time before holding a succession of political offices. He served in the US House of Representatives from Tennessee and as Tennessee's governor.

Soon after announcing his intentions to seek reelection as governor of Tennessee, his 11-week marriage ended. Instead of running for office, he decided to leave for Indian Territory (now Oklahoma) to join his adopted father, Chief Oolooteka, and his people where they had been relocated by the US government. Granted Cherokee citizenship, Houston often acted on behalf of the tribe. Later, he moved south of the Red River into the Mexican territory known as Texas. After Texas issued its Declaration of Independence, Houston was appointed a general. After his defeat of Santa Anna at San Jacinto, Houston's popularity soared.

A city was founded and named after him in 1836. The city of Houston would be capital of

Sam Houston. Library of Congress (LC-USZ62-75930)

★ Six Flags over Texas

Today when we mention "Six Flags over Texas," thoughts turn immediately to the amusement park. But the amusement park got its name from the fact that Texas has been governed by six different nations. Therefore, at different times, each of the following flags has flown over Texas: Spain, Mexico, France, Republic of Texas, the Confederate States of America, and the United States.

Texas during the first two years of the Republic. The second president, Mirabeau B. Lamar, had been the vice president under Houston. The two men frequently disagreed about how the country should be run. Houston was re-elected after Lamar's term.

It's expensive to run a country. During Houston's first term, $2 million was added to the public debt. Under Lamar, another $4.8 million was added. The Republic of Texas was deeply in debt when Houston took office for the second time. Houston tried to rein in spending. He combined, downgraded, or abolished government offices. Salaries were cut throughout state government in an effort to match income and expenditures. In his second term, he was able to keeping spending to only $511,000.

Land went for 50 cents an acre when the going rate in the rest of the United States was closer to $1.25. But people heard about the conflicts with Native Americans. Houston struggled to keep the peace between white settlers and the natives, although it was becoming harder with greedy settlers. He made treaties with native bands and avoided war with Mexico. One battle he couldn't win was the moving of the capital to Austin.

Create a Flag

Texas has been governed by six different nations: Spain, Mexico, France, the Republic of Texas, the Confederate States of America, and the United States.

Materials
★ Large piece of butcher paper cut into a rectangular shape
★ Various colors of construction paper
★ Scissors
★ Glue
★ Markers of different colors
★ ½-inch diameter wooden dowel rod

Choose an element from each of the flags pictured here. Take each of those elements to make a new flag that has a part of each of the six flags of Texas.

You may choose to draw the elements onto your new flag or you may prefer drawing them on construction paper, cutting them out, and gluing items to the new flag.

Place one end of the dowel on the side of your flag. The back of the flag should be facing upward. Fold the left edge of the paper around the rod, gluing it into place.

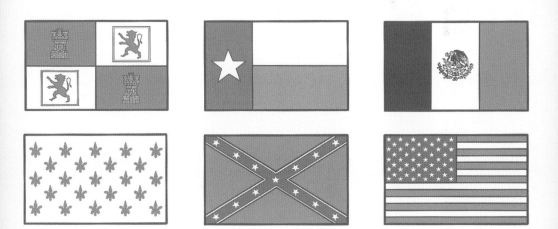

Statehood and Settlement

The Republic of Texas was an independent country for about 10 years, from 1836 to late 1845. It included present-day Texas and parts of New Mexico, Oklahoma, Kansas, Colorado, and Wyoming. It included Albuquerque, New Mexico; Dodge City, Kansas; and Rawlings, Wyoming. Approximately 7,000 more people took up residence in Texas during this time.

Growing public debt and danger from the Plains tribes and from Mexican bandits dominated Texas government. When Houston started his second term, there were many problems, particularly with the high cost of running a country. Houston and most of the Texas government knew that the answer to many of their problems was annexation by the United States. Federal assistance from the Treasury and the military would be invaluable.

Although the United States had refused to annex Texas years earlier, opinion had changed. France and England recognized Texas as an independent country. The time was right for the United States to adopt another state, the 28th state in the Union.

On July 4, 1845, the Texas legislature met to approve annexation of Texas to the United States. They created the Texas Constitution of 1845 to go along with their new role as a state of the United States. A clear and direct document, it has been called one of the best state constitutions in the country due to the straightforward manner in which it was written.

Texas Republic president Anson Jones lowered the Texas Republic flag for the last time, but when Texas raised its flag as a state, it was actually the same flag. The Lone Star flag became the state flag.

Sam Houston and Thomas J. Rusk represented Texas's interests in Washington, DC, as the new state's first US senators, and the United States sent warships to protect the Texas coast when the Mexican-American War began in 1846.

The first battle, the Battle of Palo Alto, took place north of Brownsville on May 8, 1846. The Americans were led by General Zachary Taylor and the Mexicans by General Mariano Aristo. Although the Mexican army had more than a third more troops than the United States, they also lost more men to injuries, death, and desertion. Palo Alto ended up as a standoff, but Taylor's forces had a resounding victory the next day at the Battle of Resaca de la Palma.

General Taylor reported he was happy to have Texas soldiers under his command because they were courageous and brave soldiers, but that they were too hard to control and he

Battle of Resaca de la Palma (left) and the Battle of Palo Alto (right).

never wanted to see them again. Another general, Winfield Scott, led troops into Mexico City and captured Mexico's capital. The war came to an end in 1848, two years after it started.

The United States gained land throughout the Southwest, almost half of what Mexico had claimed, according to terms of the Treaty of Guadalupe Hidalgo. But there was still land in dispute—not with Mexico, but with Texas. Texas still claimed a large part of New Mexico. In the 1850 Boundary Act, also known as the Compromise of 1850, Texas relinquished its claim to the land in exchange for $10 million to pay off old debt. Some Texans bitterly referred to it as the bribery bill.

By that time, Texas had a population of 212,000. Within 10 years, it would almost triple.

A Frontier Defense

WITH THE end of the war, government-sponsored exploration of Texas commenced. Explorers came from all fields—engineers, scientists, naturalists, artists, and military officers. The land and resources of Texas were mapped and logged. Roads were created, Indian reservations established, and towns began. And stories of their expeditions were printed in US newspapers and books. Explorers were seen as heroes, and their stories built interest in Texas.

As settlers began arriving, defense remained a very real concern. Other settlers were also traveling through Texas on their way to the California Gold Rush. One of the most dangerous parts of the trip was through Texas between San Antonio and El Paso. It was the US Army's job to protect all of these people.

A line of forts was established from the Red River to the Rio Grande to protect settlers

Fort Bliss, 7th Cavalry buildings. Library of Congress (HABS TEX,71-ELPA,7—11)

★ Camels Arrive in Texas

In 1855, Secretary of War Jefferson Davis requested an experiment using camels as "ships of the desert." It had been suggested that camels might be helpful in the dry parts of the southwestern United States. Congress authorized $30,000 to import camels for military use. The benefits were that camels could go without water for three days and could get their moisture from desert plants than no other animal would touch. And they could carry large loads.

The shipment arrived at Indianola from Egypt. After being on a ship for a while, the 33 camels seemed happy to be on sandy ground again. What the US military learned was that females were better workers, as the males were temperamental and dangerous. They crossed 120 miles in five days with no water and a temperature of 100° F in the shade. When faced with hills, the camels walked on their knees, which seemed to help their center of gravity. The main problem in using camels was that some of them ended up with sore feet.

When the Civil War came, the experiment abruptly ended. The camels escaped or were turned loose. A hundred years later, there were still occasional reports of camel sightings in the Southwest.

Frontier Diary

Frontier life, whether at a fort or a settlement, was hard. It often required that every member of the family worked, including the children. Read about frontier life for families at the PBS website for the public television series, *Frontier House*: www.pbs.org/wnet/frontierhouse /families/index.html

You might even be able to see some episodes of *Frontier House* at the PBS video site or through the classroom.

Study all these resources, and then create an alter ego who lives on the Texas frontier in the 19th century. Write a diary covering a month in the life of your frontier persona. Create at least 15 entries that capture the essence of what living the frontier life was like.

from hostile Comanche, Apache, and Kiowa. A second line of forts was built 200 miles west of the first. There weren't enough people to man the forts, even though about one-third of the US Army was stationed at Texas forts. For whatever reason, infantry units who walked or marched everywhere were sent to many forts in West Texas where horses were necessary. The forts ranged from excellent, such as Fort Bliss in El Paso, to dangerous, such as Fort Brown on the Rio Grande where soldiers suffered from multiple health epidemics—yellow fever, cholera, and dengue fever.

Conditions were rustic. Soldiers might be assigned to a fort that hadn't even been built yet, so duties were divided between building and defense. Frontier forts didn't contain just soldiers; both officers and enlisted men brought their families to these primitive conditions. Many women worked as maids, cooks,

Camp at Las Moras, Confederate States of America, near Fort Clark, Texas, March 1861.
Library of Congress (ppmsca 22783)

and laundresses, and when post hospitals became shorthanded, women were hired as nurses as well.

People living in Texas forts knew to shake out their bedding and watch where they stepped due to the presence of rattlesnakes and tarantulas. Food varied from fort to fort depending upon available resources. Housing ranged from tents to picket houses to manufactured housing. Picket houses were made from the same type of flat wood used for picket fences.

At the southern end of the line of forts was Fort Clark. A town, Las Moras, later renamed Bracketville, provided supplies for the fort and grew as the needs of the fort grew. Regiments from both the US cavalry and infantry served at Fort Clark, including the mounted regiments of African American soldiers known as Buffalo Soldiers.

Like many forts, Fort Lancaster started as a camp of canvas and prefabricated buildings, but soon adobe and stone buildings replaced the temporary camp. Fort Lancaster was manned by the First US Infantry, which was soon protecting the road from San Antonio to El Paso. Soldiers from companies H and K were called upon to escort coaches carrying passengers and the mail. The presence of the fort and its soldiers became even more important when stagecoaches began using the road in 1859.

 # Buffalo Soldiers

In 1866, Congress authorized six regiments of troops, two cavalry and four infantry, to be composed of African American soldiers. The Indians called these soldiers buffalo solders due to their curly hair, which was similar to that of buffalo. The regiments began wearing a bison on their regimental crest.

Most of the buffalo soldiers continued in the military after the Civil War because the $13 they earned each month in the military was more than they could earn in civilian life. The buffalo soldiers were stationed at the westernmost forts to keep forts and settlers safe from Indian attacks. It was a job they performed well, time and time again, despite receiving the worst of the equipment and facing discrimination. Fourteen earned the Medal of Honor during the Indian Wars, in which the military battled tribes for passage and land in westward expansion. In addition to keeping the peace, they built and renovated forts and allowed for settlement to extend into the west, whether by stagecoach, train, or telegraph.

Lieutenant Henry Flipper, the first African American graduate of West Point, served with the 10th Cavalry at Fort Concho and Fort Davis after several years in the military, and he distinguished himself as a talented engineer. Colonel William Rufus "Pecos Bill" Shafter, commanding officer at Fort Davis, relieved Flipper of quartermaster duties and later charged him with embezzlement. A court-martial hearing convicted him of "conduct unbecoming an officer and a gentleman," and had him dismissed from the US Army. Flipper went on to serve as a distinguished mining engineer in the Southwest and later became an assistant to the Secretary of the Interior. Flipper maintained his innocence through it all, and in 1999 he was posthumously pardoned by President Bill Clinton.

The forts and federal troops maintained a strong presence in Texas until the Civil War. At that time, federal troops left to fight in the war and left the forts to the Confederate army. Fort Lancaster was occupied by Walter P. Lane's Texas Rangers, but most of the forts remained empty. Some closed and never reopened. The Apaches burned most of Fort Davis.

After the Civil War, Fort Clark became an important base for Black Seminole Scouts, descendants of Seminoles and escaped slaves in the Florida everglades. In 1938, the Fort Clark commander was Colonel George S. Patton, who would later become one of the most famous generals of World War II. Fort Clark was closed in June 1944.

The Fate of Native Americans in Texas

MANY NATIVE American tribes—Cherokee, Chickasaw, Choctaw, Alabama, Coushatta—were pushed out of the southeastern United States and into Texas. They joined the Caddo, who still had a significant presence in Texas since the Spanish had viewed them as allies against the United States.

During Lamar's presidency of the Texas Republic, he took an aggressive stance against many tribes in Texas. To put it simply, he wanted them out. In June 1839, he ordered the Cherokee, Shawnee, and other tribes to leave Texas. The Cherokee, many of whom were farmers, were driven into Indian Territory, north of the Red River, but only after a devastating battle—the Battle of the Neches.

When the Cherokee were pushed from their home around Georgia after the War of 1812, the Spanish welcomed them to Texas and many settled in the northeast. Others had moved to Indian Territory on a traumatic journey known as the Trail of Tears. Texas had been their home and Sam Houston their friend. Now a vocal group of Texans wanted them out. Why? Because the Cherokee had good land, and the settlers wanted it.

The Texas troops, numbering 500, drove 700 to 800 Cherokee from their homes. The Cherokee were led by Duwali, who was better known among Texans as Chief Bowles. In addition to his Cherokee heritage, the redheaded and freckled Chief Bowles was also Scots-Irish.

Tribes remaining in Texas were ordered onto reservations in the summer of 1854. The state of Texas had made 53,000 acres of land available for two reservations. The Caddo, Waco, Anadarko, and Tonkawa tribes went to Brazos Reservation, south of Fort Belknap near the Brazos River. Each tribe had its own village and received protection from hostile bands by the federal government. Food and supplies for the reservations amounted to about $80,000 a year with arrangements for beef made with local ranchers. These tribes had a history of farming, so they grew melons, wheat, corn, and other crops. Some of the men worked for the military or the Texas Rangers as scouts.

A friendly band of Comanche, the Penateka, had land along a tributary of the Brazos about 40 miles away, the Clear Fork Reservation, also known as the upper reserve. Although the Lipan and Mescalero Apache were given land too, they never came to their assigned reservation in Texas.

Some of the white settlers in the area weren't much happier about the reservations. Native Americans traveling off the reservation were at risk of attack. Settlers attacked a leader named Choctaw Tom and his party of 17 who had permission from the government for a week's hunt. The next morning, seven were found dead and four more wounded. Governor Hardin Richard Runnels ordered Texans not to engage in hostilities with the natives and federal troops were called to investigate and protect the people on the reservations.

Everything came to a climax when rancher John Baylor led several hundred men onto the Brazos Reservation. He told troops he was looking for specific individuals, and if they fired on his party, he would also treat them as enemies. Baylor's men killed an old man and a woman working in her garden, both Native Americans. The reservation's residents pursued the men off the reservation to the Marlin Ranch a few miles away. An afternoon battle resulted in the deaths of Chief John Hatterbox and two of Baylor's men. The Brazos and Clear Fork reservations were closed and the tribes moved to Indian Territory within five years of receiving their land.

It was the Plains tribes that the Texans feared—Comanche, Apache, Kiowa, Wichita, and Tonkawa. Parker's Fort was settled by a group of strict Baptists wanting to start their own church. They arrived in Texas from Illinois in 1833 and began building a 12-foot stockade from split cedars. Two-story blockhouses in two corners were built in order to keep watch. Two rows of log cabins inside the fort became the homes of church members, including Elder John Parker, his three sons, and their families.

On the morning of May 19, 1836, most of the men were working in the fields while other adults were doing chores around their homes within the fort. Children were out playing when approximately a hundred Indians came over the hill from the east. They were mainly Comanche, but also included Kiowa and Caddo warriors as well.

One of the Parker sons, Benjamin, talked with the Indians, who asked for beef, directions to water, and a place to camp. Something about the situation must have not set well with

Benjamin because he told one of the residents, Rachel Plummer, that she should run to the woods and hide. She didn't, but lived to regret that decision.

When Benjamin returned to the Indians with beef, he was killed with a lance. Before the people of Parker's Fort could do anything, the Indians invaded the fort and killed four more settlers. Before leaving, they took five prisoners: Rachel Plummer and her son James, Elizabeth Duty Kellogg, and a brother and sister—John and Cynthia Ann Parker.

All of the captives were rescued soon except for six-year-old John Parker and nine-year-old Cynthia Anne Parker. John Parker grew up

Cynthia Parker and Prairie Flower.

with a band of Comanche and moved to Mexico as an adult.

Adopted by the Pahuka band of Comanches, Cynthia learned the language and customs of her captors until she was no longer a captive but remained of her own free will. Changing her name to Naduah, she later married Chief Peta Nocona. They had three children.

One day in 1860, a group of Texas Rangers attacked a Nawkohnees camp. One of the Comanche to die was Peta Nocona. Captain Sul Ross noticed that one of the Native Americans trying to escape had blue eyes. Realizing that she was Cynthia Anne Parker, he returned her and her infant daughter, Prairie Flower, to the Parker family in East Texas.

Cynthia was unhappy and could not adjust to life in the white world. She tried unsuccessfully to return to her Comanche family. Prairie Flower died from pneumonia within four years of joining the Parkers. Cynthia, or Naduah, died soon afterward, many said of a broken heart (but she may have starved herself).

White captives who became assimilated were somewhat common. In 1874, Lieutenant Frank Baldwin captured a white Kiowa named Tehan, a name given to him by the Kiowas and meaning "Texan." He had fair skin and red hair and was said to be a fierce warrior. He escaped from Baldwin and was never seen by authorities again.

Not all tribes moved or stayed on reservations. Raids still occurred occasionally. The Mescalero Apache had long roamed the Southwest, including West Texas. But by the 1870s, most had left for Mexico or a reservation in New Mexico. When a band of Mescalero attacked a stagecoach in Quitman County in 1881, the Texas Rangers pursued them, killing eight.

The most successful raids were led by Comanche war chief Quanah Parker. Parker, the son of Chief Nocona and Cynthia Anne Parker, slipped through the hands of army troops and Texas Rangers regularly until his band was the last free one in Texas. He was very successful for four years until the Second Battle of Adobe Walls in the Panhandle.

Quanah Parker led a Kiowa and Comanche war party of 250 against buffalo hunters staying in an abandoned trading post on June 27, 1874. One woman and 28 men defended themselves against 700 natives. The siege continued for four or five days. During that time, the hunters displayed amazing marksmanship. By the time the Indians left, three hunters and 13 Native Americans had been killed.

Afterward, authorities chased the war party. After the Civil War, the US Army renewed efforts to rid the Texas frontier of Native Americans. The US Army cracked down on all Southern Plains tribes that weren't on reservations for the next year. The series of military engagements organized by General William T. Sherman and Lieutenant General Philip H. Sheridan continued for about a year. Soldiers blocked or camped out by water sources where everyone had to come to eventually. Horses were stolen or killed. Troops would force warriors into enclosed spaces or surround them, leaving no choices except surrender or death.

Quanah Parker was the last to surrender, with 407 followers, on June 2, 1875. Along with the Kiowa and Cheyenne, the Comanche were forced onto Indian Territory. The last of the free Native Americans was removed from Texas soil.

White settlement followed, and an era of large ranches began. By 1890, the Texas frontier was gone.

Today, three reservations operate in Texas, the oldest being the Alabama-Coushatta reservation in southeast Texas with approximately 650 members. The other two are located near the Mexican border by tribes that also came after Europeans. The Kickapoos, originally from the Great Lakes, have about the same number, but use the Texas reservation mainly in winter. Many tribal members work as farm workers who travel to where they are needed in Mexico.

Today, the majority of the Texas Native American population lives in cities, but American Indian culture is celebrated in powwows from Dallas to Corpus Christi to Laredo. Festivals

Quanah Parker, Comanche chief.
Library of Congress (LC-USZ62-98166)t

Alabama-Coushatta

Interestingly, there were two tribes that Lamar didn't seek to drive out of Texas. They were the Alabama and Coushatta. In fact, he offered two leagues of land to them. Although two separate tribes, both the Alabama and Coushatta speak a similar Muskhogean language. In 1763 they also shared a desire to leave the southeast United States as settlers began moving closer. The Coushatta settled along the Trinity River, and the Alabama along the Neches River.

Spain ruled the territory then, but both tribes joined the fight for Mexican independence a few years later. The government of Mexico rewarded them with land in East Texas. When Stephen F. Austin made his map of Texas in 1829, it included the "Pueblos de los Alabamas" and the "Cusatte Village."

During the next war of independence, the provisional government of Texas sent Sam Houston to talk to the tribes in Texas. He promised land to them if they did not support Mexico. The Alabamas agreed to stay neutral, but the Coushatta supported and aided the Texans. They served as guides for the army and slaughtered their own cattle to feed the Texans driven from their homes.

Due to misunderstandings, the two tribes didn't receive their land from the Texas Republic. At the suggestion of Sam Houston, the Alabama chiefs talked to the settlers of Polk County after statehood. The citizens asked the Texas state legislature to grant 1,280 acres to the Alabama tribe. In early 1854, the Act for Relief of the Alabama Indians passed.

About 20 months later, a similar act was passed for the Coushatta, but the land never materialized. Instead, the Alabama allowed the Coushatta to join them.

In 1953, the federal legislature passed a resolution that trust relationships with Native Americans in California, Florida, New York, and Texas be dissolved. This resolution removed federal laws and benefits from those tribes. Since an agreement similar to the federal one had been made with the state of Texas, Texas tribes proceeded as always. That is, until 1981, when a game warden driving on reservation land happened to see two deer hanging in a front yard. Two men were preparing the deer meat. The game warden confiscated the deer and issued citations for hunting without a license and out of season to tribal members Lyndon Alec and Clayton Sylestine.

The tribes protested. They had always hunted on tribal land. The Polk County judge agreed and dismissed the case. However, the state's attorney general issued the opinion that the trust relationship that the tribe had enjoyed with the federal government did not exist with the state. This meant that there was no legal reservation, and that the tribes held the same legal status as a private corporation.

Texas Congressmen Ronald Coleman and Charlie Wilson requested that recognition in late 1984—the Restoration Act. It took almost three years before President Ronald Reagan signed it into law on August 18, 1987. Along the way, the Alabama-Coushatta Tribe became recognized as a single tribe.

like the St. Anthony Festival in El Paso and the Kwahadi Indian Summer Ceremonials in Palo Duro Canyon provide tradition and authentic food and dancing.

Before the 20th century, more than 50 tribes or nations resided in the state, but by 1900, the US census counted only 470 Native Americans in Texas. In 1990, there were 65,877.

European Immigration

THERE WERE many reasons for moving to Texas. But opportunities to acquire land or in industry attracted many. Land was cheap, and as long as you were prepared to work hard, you could become successful. Ranchers, farmers, investors, lumbermen, and stonemasons all arrived in Texas. So did teachers, ministers, and outlaws. Some people were looking for a little adventure, and on the Texas frontier, adventure wasn't hard to find.

Settlers arrived from Africa, Japan, Lebanon, and the Philippines. Europeans moved from Poland, Scotland, Switzerland, Belgium, France, Hungary, Greece, Czechoslovakia, and many more countries.

Norway

CLENG PEERSON (Kleng Pederson) is recognized as the father of Norse immigration to the United States. Like others in Norway, he suffered hardships in late 18th-century Norway. Peerson encouraged other Norse people to come find a better life in America. After 30 years of helping settle Norse communities in New York and the Upper Midwest, Peerson decided to settle in Texas. He and others from Norway settled in Bosque County, southwest of Fort Worth. They built homes from native limestone and named their community Norse. For a long time, it was the largest Norse community in the Southwest.

In 1982, on the 200th anniversary of Peerson's birth, King Olaf V of Norway visited Peerson's grave in Norse and the Bosque Museum that showcases a large collection of Norse artifacts, including a rocking chair made by Peerson.

Ireland

OVER HALF a million Texans claim an Irish heritage. The Irish have a long and significant immigration history to the United States, particularly Texas. Before and during the colonial period, people sometimes worked in the service of other countries, and Spain's royalty rewarded service. Christopher Columbus, an Italian, was in Spain's employ when he went sailing to the New World. A number of people from Ireland did the same. Father Michael Muldoon also worked for Spain in the early 1800s, and when Mexico won its independence, he became the priest for the Austin colony in 1831. Eight years later, he served the Republic of Texas.

Irishman Hugo O'Conor was a temporary governor of Texas when it was still a Spanish province in 1767. He started in the Spanish army in New Spain, rising to the rank of major. Because of his red hair, the Indians called him the "Red Captain." Later, while working as an inspector general, he was called to investigate a conflict between a Texas governor and a presidio commando. The governor was removed, and O'Conor became interim governor. He brought order and safety to Texas and was a popular governor.

The Irish were among the first settlers to Texas, and even were a part of Stephen Austin's successful colony. Irish colonies—Refugio and San Patricio—were set up north and west of the coastal community of Corpus Christi.

The Spanish and later the Mexican governments happily welcomed Irish colonists to Texas. The Irish were largely Catholic, like the Spanish and Mexicans, and they served as a buffer against the irritating Americans. Yet when Texans fought for their independence from Mexico, the Irish served alongside the Anglos and the Tejanos.

Twenty-five Irishmen signed the Texas Declaration of Independence at Goliad while 11 died at the Alamo. Another hundred fought under Sam Houston at San Jacinto and even provided two fifers and a drummer playing an Irish song.

Wend

EVEN WENDS of Eastern Europe settled in Texas. The Wends were a group of Slavic people who had existed since the Middle Ages, but in the 1800s, the Wends became a people without a country. They left eastern Germany in 1850. Some moved to Australia; others moved to Texas. A few years later, more came and settled near Galveston in a community they named Serbin, which continues its Wend heritage today. The native language of the Wendish people was Sorbian, although German was familiar to most due to their early time in Germany. Many of the Texas Wendish assimilated with the largest European group of Texas settlers: the Germans.

An Earthy Eden for Germans

LARGE NUMBERS of immigrants came to the United States from England, Ireland, and Scotland, but not many from Germany. That is, until Johann Friedrich Ernst came to Texas in 1831. A gardener, Ernst described the piney woods of Texas as an "earthly Eden" in a letter to a friend back home. His letters appeared in a German newspaper and a guidebook. Word spread.

Built in 1869–1870, the Anton Wulff House is in the King William Historic District approximately a half mile from present-day downtown San Antonio. Library of Congress (HABS TEX,15-SANT,24—1)

Hospital building, downtown Fredericksburg.
Karen Gibson

Large numbers of German families began moving to the Texas Hill Country. They started neighborhoods in existing cities like San Antonio and Austin; they also established new towns—Fredericksburg, Boerne, New Braunfels. These communities became part of what was called the "German belt."

They brought polka music, beer, and such customs as decorated trees at Christmas and bonfires on hills and decorated Easter eggs in spring. Today, Fredericksburg, the largest of the German towns, rings the church bells on the Saturday evening before Easter before dimming the town's lights. Dozens of bonfires are lit atop hills surrounding the city. Parents once told children that the fires were where the Easter bunny cooked the Easter eggs.

Germans also brought a strong work ethic. Many Germans were wildly successful in this new land as farmers, professors, and business owners. Alexander Sanger followed his brothers to Texas in 1872 and took over the family business. Sanger Brothers pioneered department stores in North Texas.

ACTIVITY

Make Kokosnuss Makronen

Kokosnuss Makronen (coconut macaroons) are a traditional German Christmas cookie.

Adult supervision required

Ingredients

★ ¾ cup butter

★ 1¼ cup sugar

★ 5 cups shredded coconut

★ 4 medium eggs

★ Zest from 1 lemon (the zest is the outside of the lemon; you can get the zest with a grater)

1. Preheat oven to 250°F.

2. Mix the butter, sugar, coconut, and lemon zest together in a pot set on low. Heat and stir until the butter melts.

3. Beat the eggs, adding a little of the warm coconut mixture into the eggs. Then add the eggs to the remainder of the coconut mixture. Stir slowly and heat to 120–140°F.

4. Remove pan from heat.

5. Drop 2 to 3 teaspoons of batter onto parchment paper lined cookie sheets.

6. Bake at 250°F for 20 to 25 minutes or until browned on top and edges. Remove and cool a few minutes before moving cookies to a rack to cool completely.

In 1848, Germany was experiencing a revolution like other countries in Europe. Largely, the revolutions were about middle classes insisting on more political freedom from the monarchy. In Germany, the middle class lost and huge number emigrated to the United States. In Texas, Germans prospered. They were 5 percent of the Texas population in 1850, and that number soon doubled. Within 50 years, that percentage grew to 17 percent, or approximately three million people.

Immigration began slowing down with the dawn of the 20th century. Two world wars in which Germany was the enemy led to prejudice against Germans in Texas. Germans began limiting use of the German language in newspapers, schools, and in public so as not to draw attention.

During World War I, the German Department at the University of Texas lost funding, and many people changed family and town names to sound more American. King William Street in San Antonio was renamed Pershing Avenue for a time. During World War II, Texas contained twice as many prisoner-of-war camps as any other state. The Texas camps were primarily filled with Germans.

War Comes Again

Texans expected to prosper after statehood. Instead, they spent the first five years dealing with yet another war with Mexico, boundary disputes, and continued attacks by hostile Native Americans. Still, Texas grew, and in four short years the white population doubled to over 200,000. Those who didn't emigrate from Europe largely came from the South, and the majority of those people lived in the eastern two-fifths of the state. Within 10 years, the population almost tripled.

As in the antebellum South, church tended to be the center of social life and often provided the only educational institutions as well. Methodists dominated, but there were also Baptist, Presbyterian, Catholic, Lutheran, and Episcopal churches. Southern churches were generally more evangelical in their practices than those of the North.

Southerners brought their agricultural economy with them. After working at subsistence farming, they turned their attention to developing cash crops. The most profitable cash crop of the time was cotton, sometimes referred to as King Cotton. And growing cotton went hand-in-hand with the institution of slavery.

Slavery

WHEN THE state flag first rose over Texas, there were approximately 30,000 slaves in the state—African Americans who were considered property just as much as land was. The new state constitution, written largely by men from the Old South, guaranteed the right to hold slaves. With a plantation society in place, the eastern half of Texas began to resemble the antebellum South more than the western frontier.

The slave population grew even faster than the free population. By 1860, slaves accounted for 30 percent of the population. In some counties, the percentage was even higher. In Brazoria County near Houston, slaves made up 72 percent of the population.

Most of the slaves in Texas had moved to the state with their owners. Nearby New Or-leans was the main port for Africans brought to America as slaves, although up to 2,000 came straight to Texas through the Galveston and Houston ports annually. The price for the average slave doubled from $400 in 1850 to $800 in 1860. Young adult field hands and skilled slaves cost the most, from $1,200 to $2,000. Field hands worked from sunrise to sundown on plantations, while skilled laborers lived in towns and worked as mechanics, blacksmiths, and day laborers. Skilled laborers and house servants were considered favored positions—they received better treatment and more freedom than field slaves.

Slaves typically lived in small log cabins with dirt floors, cooking dinners of pork, wild game, and fish in the fireplace. Many grew vegetables to supplement their food, with sweet potatoes a particular favorite. Clothing and shoes made from coarse materials rarely fit right, and medical care was almost nonexistent. Marriage and families were encouraged as a way to control slaves. Perhaps it was the threat that families could be broken up at any time that made family life so important. Churches used music and song not only to show devotion to God but also as a means of expressing what could not be said out loud in day-to-day life.

Some slaves ran away. Many slaves feared that the high price being advertised for the return of runaway slaves made capture almost certain. Fear of being caught by slave patrols or being split from children and family members kept many from running away.

Regardless, some situations were unbearable, and African Americans did run away. The most successful were those who escaped to Mexico, which had long outlawed the institution of slavery. African Americans who didn't run away dreamed of the day they could be free.

Slavery and religion were just part of the widening gulf between the South and the North, which turned to talk of secession (withdrawing from the Union). While Texas had adopted many Southern practices, not everyone supported the idea of secession. Sam Houston, still a popular Texas politician, believed that the Union should stay whole. Houston ran for governor again in 1859. His opponent was the incumbent governor, Hardin Richard Runnels, who had actually beat Houston in the 1857 gubernatorial race. The 1859 election was bitter. Runnels ran on a strongly pro-Southern platform. Houston won—36,277 to 27,500. Runnel's loss was due in part to Houston's popularity, but some of his policies as governor hasn't gone over well.

"When Texas united her destiny with that of the United States, she entered not into the North, nor South. Her connection was not sectional, but national," Houston said in his inaugural address, in which he hoped to discourage

Write a Slave Narrative Profile

Many projects use oral and written narratives to capture the history and essence of a time period. You can hear some memories of slavery at www.pbs.org/wnet/slavery/memories/index_flash.html.

In the 1930s, the Works Progress Administration funded a Federal Writers' Project dedicated to chronicling the experience of slavery. Former slaves were interviewed, and

Ellen Butler, former slave, Beaumont
Library of Congress (LC-USZ62-125194)

those interviews were transcribed. A list of sample interview transcriptions are listed at http://newdeal.feri.org/asn/asn00.htm. Choose an interview for a former slave from Texas, such as James Green.

After reading the interview, create a character sketch. A character sketch is a way of introducing or describing another person. Based on what you've read and what you infer, answer the following questions.

1. Describe the physical appearance of the character. What does his/her experience say about that person?

2. What is the subject's background? Home? Family? Education?

3. Describe the subject's personality.

4. What kind of language does the subject us? What does the language or way of speaking tell you?

5. What past experiences have influences the subject and how?

After you have answered the questions, write a one to two page paper introducing your subject to someone else.

the idea of seceding. He had also discouraged secession while serving as US senator.

While Texans chose the moderate candidate for their state leader, they went in the other direction for a US senator two months later, choosing Louis T. Wigfall, a vocal secessionist and enemy of Houston. In the 1860 Democratic Convention, Runnels was part of an ultra-Southern group who opposed the nomination of Northern Democrat Stephen A. Douglas for president. Many Southern delegations walked out of the convention, nominating their own candidate, John C. Breckinridge. The Constitutional Union Party considered nominating Sam Houston but went with John Bell of Tennessee instead. These candidates would be running against the Republican candidate, Abraham Lincoln.

The election of Abraham Lincoln would not do, according to slave-owning Texans, and Lincoln received no votes in Texas. Breckinridge won in Texas against Bell by a 3-to-1 margin. Lincoln still won the election, and South Carolina became the first state to secede on December 20, 1860. Like dominoes falling, five more states seceded in January.

Most Texans weren't slave owners, but often the richest Texans were. Texans who came from the Deep South often favored slavery whether they held slaves or not. Texas became a state divided after Lincoln's election.

A series of fires broke out in North Texas during the summer of 1860, burning parts of downtown Dallas and Denton in what the newspapers called the Texas Troubles. It was hot summer where temperatures of 110° F were reported. Citizens in Denton decided "prairie matches" were to blame for the fires. The matches, made from phosphorus, weren't stable and could spontaneously combust. Others decided abolitionists and slaves were to blame, and vigilantes threatened revenge. Approximately 100 people were killed that summer.

Anthony Bewley, a Methodist minister in Fort Worth, had argued against slavery. When things began to worsen, he feared for his family and left for Kansas. He was caught and returned to Fort Worth. A lynch mob hung him.

Texas Secedes

SAM HOUSTON told legislators that the Civil War would bring nothing but bloodshed and destruction to Texas. The state legislature called a special session, and on February 1, 1861, voted to secede from the Union, becoming the seventh state to do so. Houston refused Lincoln's offer of federal troops, not wanting to create a civil war in Texas. But when Houston refused to take an oath of loyalty to the Confederate States of America, he was removed from office.

Houston retired from political life. One of his sons, Sam Houston Jr., joined the Confederate army against his father's wishes and was wounded in battle. In 1863 at the age of 70, Sam Houston died of pneumonia as the Civil War raged around him.

The Civil War

On April 12, 1861, at 4:30 am, the beginning shots of the Civil War were fired at Fort Sumter, South Carolina. In Texas, recruiting for volunteer troops had already begun. By the end of the year, about 25,000 Texans had joined the Confederate army—mostly the cavalry because Texans preferred riding horses to walking, as required of the infantry.

Recruitment became more difficult as the war dragged on, prompting the Confederate Congress to require military service for men between the ages of 18 and 35. The age range eventually increased to 17 to 50 years.

The number of Texans in the Confederate army eventually totaled approximately 90,000 with the majority protecting the state from Union invasion and Native American attacks. Part of their role was to expand the Confederacy into New Mexico Territory, but Texas troops engaged with Union troops as well. Colonel William C. Young and the Eleventh Texas Cavalry crossed the Red River in May 1861 and

 Secession Today

Think of secession as a thing of the past? Think again. States have seceded to form new states, as in the case of West Virginia and Virginia. And at the time of this writing, counties in northern Colorado are petitioning to become their own state as well.

In 2012, there was talk of Texas seceding from the Union once more when Texas railroad commissioner Barry Smitherman stated that Texas had the resources to operate as an independent nation. And it's true that Texas has many resources. For energy, Texas has 25 percent of the nation's oil reserves and 33 percent of the natural gas. With its 16 ports, foreign exports totaled $265 billion in 2011 and the gross domestic product was $1.2 trillion.

However, history shows that when Texas tried to function as its own country once before, it didn't go well. The costs of running a government are immense and include creating a military, setting up trade agreements, and paying for it all. Regardless, according to the Supreme Court after the Civil War, secession now requires the consent of other states or an act of Congress.

captured federal forts Arbuckle, Cobb, and Washita.

Other maneuvers involving Texas troops included limiting Union movement into Arkansas and Louisiana with troops stationed in Indian Territory (later Oklahoma). Some of these brigades and batteries included Native Americans from Indian Territory in the troops. These areas were important. If the Union gained a foothold in either state, it would just be a matter of time before they invaded northeast Texas.

Private Thomas F. Bates of D Company, 6th Texas Infantry Regiment, with Bowie knife and John Walch pocket revolver. Library of Congress

(LC-DIG-ppmsca-32600)

Other Texan soldiers crossed the Mississippi River to fight. The Texas Brigade, commanded by General John Bell Hood, fought at Gettysburg and the Battle of Chickamauga, a great victory for the Confederacy. Confederate general Robert E. Lee was relieved to see reinforcements from the Texas Brigade at the Battle of the Wilderness. The Texas Brigade was ordered to the front of the line to hold off the Union, which they did.

The Eighth Texas Cavalry, better known as Terry's Texas Rangers, became well known on the battlefields of Georgia, Kentucky, Mississippi, Tennessee, and North and South Carolina. Formed in Houston by Colonel Benjamin Franklin Terry, the regiment was recognized by many a Union solider.

Defending the Texas coastline was perhaps the most important mission. Brigadier General Earl Van Dorn organized the coastal defense. Forts were fortified and heavy cannons added. The Union Navy appeared off the coast in November 1861, firing at Confederate troops at Aransas Pass, Indianola, and Port Lavaca. The CSS *Royal Yacht*, a Confederate patrol schooner, was burned as well.

Union efforts only intensified in the next year as they attacked coastal communities like Corpus Christi. A navy blockade made it almost impossible for ships from foreign countries to get through. Texas, which had long done business with foreign countries, was cut off from the rest of the world except for the few blockade runners that were able to sail cotton out of Texas and return with goods and guns.

The largest seaport in Texas was Galveston. Successfully capturing Galveston would be a feather in the Union cap, and on October 4, 1862, forces decided to do just that when they approached the port. Confederate artillery spotted Union forces and fired. But they were no match for the Union's firepower. The Union captured Galveston.

Texans don't give up easily, though. General John Bankhead Magruder quickly made plans to recapture Galveston. Timing and strategy were key. For timing, Magruder decided on 1:00 AM on New Year's Day 1863 while federal troops slept. Confederate land forces moved across the railroad bridge from the mainland at night while two river steamers-turned-gunboats glided through the dark harbor toward the Union warships. When the order to attack commenced, land troops quickly captured the Union infantry.

On water, the battled waged on as the gunboats, the CSS *Neptune* and the CSS *Bayou City*, attacked the much larger federal ships. The USS *Harriet Lane* sank the *Neptune*, but the troops from the *Bayou City* boarded and captured the ship. Another federal ship ran aground at Pelican Spit, while the commander

of another detonated his ship rather than let Confederates capture it. The explosion took the life of the commander and 14 crew members. The remaining Union ships made their escape to open water, and Texas celebrated the return of Galveston.

The Union Navy renewed its efforts to capture Galveston. The plan of Major General Nathaniel P. Banks was to land at Sabine Pass and overtake Galveston from inland. Sabine Pass wasn't seen as a problem as there was only a small fort with 47 soldiers commanded by a local Irish barkeeper. Four Union gunboats fired on the fort. The Confederates returned fire with alarming skill. In 35 minutes, the Confederates fired 107 rounds from its six cannons, putting two of the gunboats out of commission and capturing their crews.

What the Union couldn't do in Galveston, they were able to accomplish in Brownsville, at the southernmost point of the Texas coast at the mouth of the Rio Grande. This cut off trade between Texas and its nearest trade partner, Mexico. However, when many Union troops were transferred to Louisiana in the spring of 1864, Confederate Texans were able to recapture Brownsville. The only area that the Union was able to hold onto was Brazos Island.

The governor, Francis R. Lubbock, was so committed to the Confederacy that he spent

View of Indianola. Library of Congress (pga 03929)

the first half of the war raising troops and funds for the cause. But by December 1863, he thought his efforts would be put to better use behind the front line, and he joined the Confederate military.

Not all Texans supported the Confederacy, but those Texans who supported the Union learned to be quiet about it. Union support was found in the German Hill Country and north of Dallas. Texas Germans issued a resolution declaring slavery to be evil, which led to mistrust from other Texans. When 65 mainly German Union sympathizers tried to leave the state, they engaged in conflict with state Confederate troops at the Nueces River and 35 members were killed.

Other people supporting the Union left the state, either to join the Union army or to feel safer in Union territory. Approximately 2,132 whites and 47 African Americans from Texas joined the Union army.

Unlike other Southern states, life didn't change drastically for many Texans during the Civil War. The blockades resulted in a shortage of items such as clothing, medicine, and coffee. This was particularly bad when the Union was in control of Brownsville and Texas couldn't get items from Mexico. Coffee was missed by many, but some creative folks tried to create substitutes from peanuts, corn, okra, or sweet potatoes. Newspapers published erratically due to a shortage of paper to print on. Farmers moved from growing cotton to growing corn and other crops to feed the troops.

Other businesses started due to war needs. Cannon foundries, percussion-cap factories, and textile miles were important businesses for maintaining the Confederacy.

In April 1865, word began filtering into Texas that General Robert E. Lee had surrendered. But Texas had one more battle left to fight, the Battle of Palmito Ranch. The four-hour battle resulted in only a few dozen wounded Confederate soldiers. On the Union side, there were 30 wounded and 111 Union

★ Texas in Wartime

When Camp Logan opened in Houston for training purposes and to protect the Gulf area during World War I, instead of fighting a foreign enemy, white soldiers fought against the African American Third Battalion stationed at the camp. Martial law was declared when a riot erupted.

The 90th Division of the US Army, better known as the Tough 'Ombres, came from Camp Travis in Texas. They fought in France during World War I. In World War II, the unit was reactivated and returned to Europe to fight in battles including D-Day. The Tough 'Ombres lost almost 3,000 men in the line of duty.

Also in World War II, Texan Audie Murphy won almost every medal there was. Murphy came from a small northeast Texas farming community called Farmersville. He wrote a book about his adventures called *To Hell and Back*. It was later made into a movie.

soldiers killed. When word spread that leaders throughout the Confederacy were surrendering, some Texas political and military leaders escaped to Mexico when Generals Smith and Magruder issued the terms of surrender.

Juneteenth

ONE MORE important group needed to be told, and it took a Union general fortified by Union forces to deliver the message. General Gordon Granger arrived in Galveston on June 19, 1865, to let 250,000 African American Texans know that the Union had won, and that they were free. He read the Emancipation Proclamation Lincoln had delivered two and a half years earlier.

An annual celebration that became known as Juneteenth continues today with ceremonies, entertainment, picnics, and family reunions. Early Juneteenth celebrations often concentrated on teaching African Americans about their rights, particularly voting rights. In 1979, Texas made Juneteenth a state holiday. Many communities have Emancipation Parks where the annual celebrations take place. Ceremonies often open with the hymn "Lift Every Voice."

The Civil War may have ended and resulted in freedom from slavery, but in Texas and elsewhere, African Americans still fought for many years for basic rights—voting, education, and basic safety.

Lincoln reading the Emancipation Proclamation. Library of Congress (LC-DIG-pga-02502)

Racial riots have broken out from time to time. The Longview Race Riot was one of 25 riots during the summer of 1919. Fighting broke out between white and black residents of the town. Governor William Hobby sent in Texas Rangers and the National Guard to keep the peace. Although men from both sides were arrested, nobody was ever convicted. Martial law was declared in Beaumont after a 1943 race riot. Three people died, and more than 200 were arrested.

African American children were first exposed to education through church-sponsored

Plan a Juneteenth Celebration

Juneteenth celebrates the ending of slavery in America, but it also celebrates African American culture. Plan your own Juneteenth celebration. Go to www.Juneteenth.com for ideas. Often General Order No. 3 is read aloud:

The people of Texas are informed that, in accordance with a proclamation from the Executive of the United States, all slaves are free. This involves an absolute equality of personal rights and rights of property, between former masters and slaves and the connection heretofore existing between them, becomes that between employer and hired labor. The Freedmen are advised to remain at their present homes and work for wages. They are informed that they will not be allowed to collect at military posts; and they will not be supported in idleness either there or elsewhere.

Start the celebration with a public reading of General Order No. 3 and/or the Emancipation Proclamation. Have participants share what those words mean to them personally.

Emancipation Day Celebration, 1900.

Wikipedia Commons

schools. Later segregation in public schools was contested, and the US Supreme Court ruled that schools must be integrated, a law that would be tested time and time again. Thelma Joyce White was denied admission into Texas Western College (now the University of Texas at El Paso) in 1954.

Although the University of Texas Medical Branch in Galveston admitted its first African American student in 1949, UT's law school had to be ordered to racially integrate. Once the Supreme Court decision was made, a judge stated that the University of Texas could not deny admission based on race.

Another federal court decision ordered the Mansfield School District to integrate in 1956. When three black students tried to enroll in Mansfield High School in 1956, a mob prevented it. Demonstrations and continued resistance led Governor Allan Shivers to transfer the students to Fort Worth. The next year state segregation laws were passed that delayed integration for years.

Texas had African American communities, such as Mosier Valley. The Mosier Valley school was part of the Euless School District. The school superintendent tried to bus the children to schools in Fort Worth in 1950 as the Mosier Valley school was falling apart. Parents fought the bussing decision, and US district judge Joe Dooley ruled that students had the right to be educated in their own district and would have to go to the all-white Euless school. When the families tried to enroll, they were denied and told that segregation laws overrode education laws. A new Mosier Valley school was built and served the African American community until 1968 when the Euless school system was finally integrated.

The Texas state legislature did its best with various laws to keep African Americans from voting. In 1923, the Texas legislature passed legislation barring African Americans from voting in Democratic primaries. In 1924, physician and civil rights advocate Lawrence Aaron Nixon was denied a ballot in El Paso. For 20 years, he fought for his right to vote, and finally won after the US Supreme Court ruled on African American voting rights.

While progress has been made, the current voter identification laws in Texas have been called discriminatory to African Americans.

Reconstruction

THERE WERE no celebrations in the rest of Texas. President Andrew Johnson declared peace in the original 10 Confederate states on April 2, 1866. Over four months later, peace was declared with Texas.

Not all Texans accepted defeat easily. James Webb Throckmorton was the governor of Texas when peace was declared by the United States, but within a year, he was removed from office for refusing to support Reconstruction or the Fourteenth Amendment that freed slaves.

But Texas did move on, approving a new constitution. The following year, Texans elected their first Republican governor and 14 African Americans to the state legislature.

Texas Democrats were unhappy with a constitution that outlawed slavery and centralized the state government. On September 6, 1875, the Constitutional Convention was held in Austin. While the new constitution couldn't allow for slavery, it did place restrictions on state finances, including expenditures, taxes, and debt. State banks were abolished, and corporations received limitations in how to operate. The Constitution of 1876, approved by voters in February 1876, remains in effect today.

The last and final capitol building, constructed from Texas red granite, was completed in 1888 after 10 years of construction. The Renaissance Revival style is based on 15th-century Italian architecture. It is the largest in square footage of all state capitols, and the tallest of any state capitol, including the US Capitol in Washington, DC.

32nd Annual Conference of the National Association for the Advancement of Colored People (NAACP), Houston, June 24–28, 1941.
Library of Congress (LC-USZ62-111536)

Home on the Range

Early Texas travelers had only four choices when they needed to get from one town to another: walk, ride a horse, bounce along in a buggy, or take a stagecoach.

Stagecoach is a general term for a horse-drawn wagon that carries passengers, but there were two main types. The traditional coach, resembling a teacup on four wheels, was actually a Concord coach, invented by Lewis Downing and J. Stephen Abbot from Concord, New Hampshire. The Concord coach, pulled by four to six horses, was usually red with yellow trim and gold scroll and paintings on the doors. Various sizes accommodated from 6 to 12 passengers. Most passengers sat on red upholstered seats inside the coach, but others might ride on top with the driver.

Another type of coach was the celerity coach or mud wagon. This lighter wagon could travel faster and was more useful on roads less traveled, such as those found in West Texas. A canvas tarp could be rolled up or tied down depending on the weather. Celerity coaches were often drawn by mules.

Stagecoach

TEXAS'S FIRST regularly scheduled public transportation, made up of horse-drawn stagecoaches, started soon after Texas won its independence from Mexico. A year after the Battle of San Jacinto, a stage line connected Houston to Harrisburg, five miles away. The next year, travelers could get from Houston to Washington-on-the-Brazos in 30 hours. Every Thursday at 6:00 AM, the stagecoach left the Houston House Inn. On Wednesdays, travelers could catch the coach to Houston.

Passengers arriving in Texas by ship would board the stagecoach at Galveston's Planter House to reach Austin, New Braunfels, or another destination.

Stage lines depended on mail contracts and demand. Mail delivery started with 15 routes

Celerity stagecoach. Library of Congress (LC-USZ62-33494)

between the most populated areas of the eastern half of Texas. Originally, mail was delivered by horseback, but there was only so much that could be carried on a horse.

Stagecoaches were then set up to deliver mail. Most coaches started with a government mail contract. Adding passengers just added to the profit. As most coaches carried mail, payment might be reflected on the length of time it took for delivery. Because of this, most early coaches stopped every 15 to 30 miles to change horses. Less often, there might be a change in drivers. Passengers might have the opportunity for a quick meal during these stops.

On particularly long trips, an overnight stay or a longer meal might be provided. Both accommodations and meals varied widely at stage stops. A stop might be an elegant inn or a shack next to a corral. It could also be a tent.

Meals cost from 40 cents to a dollar. The Sargent Hotel, the stage stop in Brackettville, was a stop travelers enjoyed because the proprietor offered hot cakes and coffee. A good dinner at a stage stop was wild game with either biscuits or cornbread and washed down with sweet milk—unpasteurized whole milk—or coffee. But travelers were just as likely to come away from a stage stop with a chunk of greasy meat and wormy biscuits.

Popular stage lines were Austin to San Antonio and Houston to Austin. Both were provided by the Austin firm of Risher & Sawyer. The Austin–San Antonio trip occurred three times a week. The 75-mile trip took 18 hours on a good day.

During the heat of the summer, particularly when a stage was traveling in West Texas, travelers might have to rise at 2:00 AM in order to avoid the hottest part of the day. When bad weather struck, it could take up to a week and passengers might have to get out and push the coach out of the mud. A Concord stage named the *General Sam Houston* added two more horses or mules to the six it already used when there was mud to travel through.

The first to provide service out of state was frontiersman Henry Skillman, who provided service from San Antonio to El Paso to Santa Fe in 1851. Birch used 400 horses and mules and 65 drivers for 50 stages. The 1,476-mile trip took about 27 days. Passengers paid about $200 for a one-way trip. Mules were most effective, traveling farther and needing less water. Because of this, the trip soon enjoyed the nickname "the Jackass Mail."

In 1849, gold was discovered in California. Suddenly, a lot of people had gold fever and wanted to get to California as soon as possible. Demand rose for transcontinental transportation. The demand was initially met by John Butterfield, who contracted with the US Post Office to provide twice-a-week mail services for $600,000 a year. The contract also stated that the trip had to be made in 24 days.

The Butterfield Overland Mail Co.'s 2,795-mile route started in St. Louis, traveled 740 miles in Texas, and ended in San Francisco. The Texas part of the trip took about eight days to travel.

New York Herald reporter Waterman L. Ormsby rode out with the first Butterfield stage on September 16, 1858. He wrote about the trip, "I now know what Hell is like. I've just had 24 days of it."

Stagecoach rides were less than comfortable. Passengers were bounced around. A *San Antonio Herald* editor wrote, "to make excellent jam, squeeze six or eight women, now-a-days, into a common stagecoach."

Stagecoaches were also targets for attacks from hostile Native Americans and bandits. In fact, it became expected that you would be robbed by a masked man if you traveled on a

 ## The End of the Stagecoach

Stagecoaches continued to entertain long after they stopped being functional. Buffalo Bill Cody used a Concord stagecoach in his Wild West shows, even when he took the shows overseas. There was also a demand for stagecoaches by movie producers of westerns. The title of a famous 1939 film directed by John Ford was *Stagecoach*. It starred John Wayne.

coach. Some people actually felt let down when they didn't have that experience. Some robbers had Robin Hood reputations; those who didn't rob women were considered gentlemen.

Overland Mail Co. lost more than 50 employees in Texas attacks by Kiowa and Comanche. The ability of a driver to protect the passengers and cargo was important. One famed driver was a former Texas Ranger, William A. "Bigfoot" Wallace.

Less than six weeks before the Civil War started, the route for the Overland Mail Co. (Butterfield was no longer a part of the company) was moved north and no longer went through Texas. Texas still had 31 stage lines running. Half were owned the Austin businessman Risher and a new partner C. K. Hall.

After the war, the number of stagecoaches and routes increased in Texas, but only for a short time. The stagecoach had competition. The railroad had arrived.

Railroads Come to Texas

IF YOU were a passenger in a 19th-century stagecoach looking out a window, you might see iron rails being laid out near the same road you were taking. Railroads nipped at the heels of the stagecoach. Like coaches, railroads began appearing before the Civil War. Unlike the stagecoach, nothing continued during the war. In fact, there was no building for seven years, plus the wood from the railways was pulled up to use in building forts.

Railroads opened the United States for settlement faster than anything had before. The web of tracks with their "iron horses" also made it possible to ship things across the country in a fraction of the time. The immense size of Texas made railroads a logical step for transportation.

Railroad entrepreneurs wanted the state to pay for the building of railroads for the private corporations. Some Texas politicians resisted, believing that if Texas was going to build the railroads, they should own them as well. It was a political battle that the railroad owners won. In 1856, the Texas legislature authorized $6,000 to railroad companies, but construction was slow in getting started. By 1860, 400 miles of railroad was in use, almost all of it coming out of Houston. The Galveston, Houston and Henderson railroad traveled between Houston and Galveston. The Texas and New Orleans line traveled from Houston to Orange, Texas, on the border of Louisiana. Houston became a railway center with tracks leading out in five different directions.

In 1870, the Texas legislature granted the Missouri-Kansas-Texas Railroad, better known

The opening of the Louisiana and Texas Railroad in 1876. Library of Congress (LC-USZ62-24752)

as the Katy, a charter to build a railroad in the state. It was the first to come from the north, approaching through Denison, on Christmas Day 1872. The company advertised the Katy as the "Gateway to Texas."

Stagecoaches continued to operate in Texas wherever trains didn't go. However, two towns in West Texas had both. The man who ran a stage line from Albany to Cisco competed against the Houston & Texas Central train that made the same trip. The irregular service of the train made the stagecoach the better option for some time.

The last stagecoach to operate as public transportation on a regularly scheduled trip was the trip from Alice to Brownsville, a 36-hour trip. A stage, pulled by four horses, left Alice each day at 6:00 AM until 1904 when the St. Louis, Brownsville and Mexico Railroad came to town. The people of Brownsville were now connected to Memphis, St. Louis, and Chicago. The railroad was even responsible for creating a town. The owner of King Ranch gave 75,000 acres for the railroad right-of-way and 640 acres for a town. Kingsville was born, and the railroad opened its headquarters there. Although it started as a railroad town, Kingsville added a trade center, naval air station, and a college, and became the county seat.

By 1888, Texas had more than 8,000 miles of railroad with more track going down all the time. Two transcontinental routes spanned the state. Things didn't always go well, though. In 1896, the Katy Railroad decided on a publicity stunt 15 miles north of Waco. They created a "town" called Crush and then staged a "Crash at Crush." The plan was to have two train engines crash into each other head-on.

On the day of the crash, more than 40,000 people came to watch. A red engine and a green engine started four miles from each other. Each traveled two miles until they crashed head-on, leading to a fire and flying debris that killed three people and injured more.

Trailing the railroad was the telegraph. The telegraph was first introduced in 1832. The inventor, Samuel F. B. Morse, offered its use to the Republic of Texas during Lamar's term, but received no answer. It wasn't until January 5, 1854, that the first telegraph started in Texas— the Texas and Red River Telegraph Company. The office in Marshall allowed people to send messages to various locations in Louisiana and to Natchez, Mississippi. The same year, wire was strung connecting Galveston and Houston with other Texas towns. The first permanent telegraph line was between Galveston and Houston.

Telegrams for less than 25 miles cost a quarter. The *Galveston News* was the first newspaper to use the telegraph as way to get the news faster in order to share with readers.

The Texas Rangers

WHEN STEPHEN Austin was starting the colonies in Texas, he knew that many dangers awaited them on the Texas frontier. He hired 10 frontiersmen to protect the settlers. Within three years, the number increased to between 20 and 30. These lawmen handled anything—robberies, murder, vandalism. The Texas-Mexico border was the site of frequent problems, known as the "Bandit Wars," and the rangers were often the only law.

The Texas Ranger became a special state law officer called in for bigger problems. If there was an attack by hostile Native Americans, the Texas Rangers tracked the war party until they were caught. Rangers might be called in to settle family feuds, political disputes, and gunfights. During wartime, the rangers served as scouts and spies.

They became legendary. Captain John Coffee Hays and 13 of his men were once ambushed by 70 Comanche. Carrying the new Colt repeating pistol, Hays led the Rangers through the Comanche with guns blazing.

The Rangers participated in many gunfights, but if they could capture the bad guy, they might just take him to Judge Roy Bean, known as the "Law West of the Pecos." Bean was known to come up with unique judicial

Texas Rangers captain John Coffee Hays.
Library of Congress (LC-USZ62-83948)

 Texas Treasury Robbed

One crime the Texas Rangers were unable to solve was the robbery of the state treasury in the spring of 1865. It was a hectic time in the South with the downfall of the Confederacy. But General Nathan G. Shelley got word that thieves were coming to the treasury in Austin. George R. Freeman, leader of the volunteer militia, arrived with 20 troops while the robbers were still in the building. A gunfight started, and one robber was killed. The rest were last seen riding west of Austin toward Mount Bonnel. They made off with approximately $17,000. Half of it was in silver and gold. The robbers were never caught nor was the money ever recovered.

decisions, such as fining a corpse for carrying a concealed weapon. The $40 fine paid for the man's funeral expenses.

Outlaws kept the Texas Rangers busy after the Civil War. Some of these criminals started out as Confederate irregulars from Missouri. When Belle Starr's family moved to Texas, they gave the outlaws shelter until Belle Starr started committing her own crimes as the "Bandit Queen."

Other Texas outlaws include Bill Longley and Sam Bass. Bass arrived in Texas at the age of 19 and tried different occupations without much luck. He had better success robbing stagecoaches and trains. In 1878, he robbed four trains within 25 miles of each other. He was pursued by Texas Rangers and died in a gunfight.

No Texas outlaws were as notorious as Bonnie and Clyde. Bonnie Parker was 19 when she met Clyde Barrow during the Great Depression. They started their life of crime in the Dallas area—stealing cars, kidnapping, and robberies, including a National Guard armory. They were responsible for at least 13 deaths.

Texas Ranger Frank Hamer arranged a roadside ambush outside Gibsland, Louisiana. Bullets rained on the crooked couple—167 of them. Their bodies were put on public display in Dallas before burial in their family plots.

Bonnie and Clyde. Wikimedia Commons

The Texas Ranger Division still operates today as an arm of the Texas Department of Public Safety. There are approximately 150 agents responsible for criminal investigations in major crimes, unsolved crime/serial crime investigations, public corruption investigations, reviewing officer-involved shootings, and handling border security issues.

Actors John Wayne and Chuck Norris were named honorary Texas Rangers.

Cattle Drives and the Cowboy

THE CATTLE industry led to different types of criminals for the Texas Rangers to apprehend—cattle thieves and fence cutters. Cattle thieves would sell the stolen cattle and make money. Sometimes it was even a family operation, as when John Short and his family were part of a cattle theft operation. John's older son was hanged, and his son-in-law became the first inmate at the Texas State Penitentiary. John's youngest son, 16-year-old Thomas Short, confessed to cattle theft in 1849 but was acquitted because of his age.

Fence cutting was a new crime. For years, Texas ranchers operated with free-grass or open-range cattle. Some ranches realized that a fence

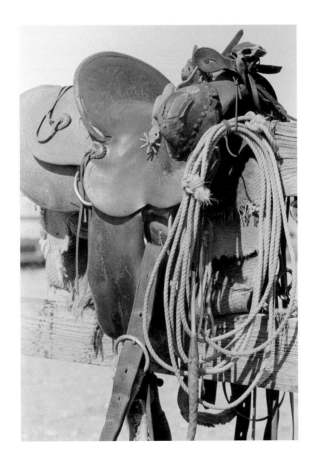

Detail of a cowboy's saddle.

would reduce the need to watch over cattle to make sure they didn't wander off, and it would certainly make cattle theft a little harder.

In September 1883, open-range ranchers cut the fence at Mabel Day's ranch. Her 85,000-acre ranch was the first large ranch that was totally fenced. The open-range/free-grass proponents not only believed that cattle should have access to grass, but it was also a drought year and Day's ranch had water sources.

Day's ranch was saddled with debt and now she had miles of fence to repair. But she began lobbying the Texas legislature to make fence cutting a felony. The law passed in 1884, and the Texas Rangers were kept busy for a number of years.

Ranches weren't anything new in Texas. Once the Spanish realized there were no golden cities, ranching became one of the first industries in Texas. The number and size of ranges made ranching a golden opportunity in the right hands. One of those with the right hands was Captain Richard King. As an 11-year-old boy, King was indentured to a New York City jeweler. The jeweler was a difficult man to work for, never satisfied.

King stowed away on a ship and headed south. A hard worker, King learned the steamboating business in Alabama and Florida. Before long, he owned his own business and was a steamboat captain. He set up a steamboat business in Texas, moving goods and people along the lower Rio Grande.

During his travels, King became acquainted with a South Texas area known as Wild Horse Desert. He noticed that wildlife was plentiful and that there was plenty of water. If wildlife could thrive, so could domestic livestock. With his partner, Gideon "Legs" Lewis, King purchased a Mexican land grant, the 15,500-acre Rincon de Santa Gertrudis, in 1852.

King developed his ranch based on the Southern plantation and the Mexican hacienda system. He added to his holdings, and the ranch grew. Although the ranch was remote, it developed a reputation as a place of refinement for travelers, thanks to King's wife, Henrietta.

Due to the ranch's location in the Rio Grande valley, many of King's workers came from Mexico. It was reported that he moved the inhabitants of a Mexican village suffering from drought to his ranch and employed them. They became known as *kineños*, "King's men."

King raised various livestock—cattle, sheep, goats, and horses. He had the greatest success with cattle and horses. He crossed Brahman bulls with shorthorns to produce Santa Gertrudis cattle, recognized as its own breed in

Riders at the King Ranch.
Library of Congress (LC-DIG-highsm-14160)

73

Design a Ranch Brand

To the untrained eye, there might not be much difference in the appearance of various cows, so you might wonder how anyone would know which livestock belonged to which rancher, particularly if they were open-range cattle. Ranchers solved this by branding their livestock. For example, the brand at the King Ranch is called the Running W. It's a wavy W. Some say the brand represents the often-seen diamondback rattlesnakes on the ranch. Others say that the wave pattern represents continuity between the past and the future.

Letters, numbers, and symbols have all been used as in brands for livestock. The best brands say something about the owner. Design your own unique brand.

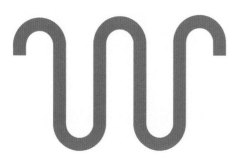

Adult supervision required

Materials

★ Paper
★ Pencil
★ Fine-tip marker
★ Square or rectangular eraser
★ Artist's knife or utility knife
★ Ink pad
★ Adult helper

1. Sketch some ideas for brands on paper. Experiment with different letters, numbers, or symbols that represent you or that are important to you.

2. When you've decided on your brand, use the fine tip marker to draw it on the eraser.

3. With adult assistance, use the knife to carve away everything except the design.

4. When you are ready to stamp your brand on something, just press the brand onto the ink pad and then onto your personal belonging.

1940. Also in the 1940s, the King Ranch began breeding and racing both thoroughbreds and quarter horses. They even had a Triple Crown winner in 1946 with After Assault.

The ranch branched out into oil leases, mineral recovery, farming, and the timber industry. Today, the King Ranch is one of the largest ranches in the world, and continues to be so among the top 200 businesses in Texas.

What changed for the Texas rancher were the cattle drives of the late 19th century. Although cattle were occasionally moved to Midwestern markets, the practice had largely stopped during the Civil War. After the war, the demand for beef in the North and the East was tremendous.

Longhorn steer. Karen Gibson

Slaughterhouses would pay $40 a head. Trains were well established in Kansas and St. Louis, so all the ranchers had to do was get the cattle to Kansas.

Ranchers hired men to drive the cattle to the markets. Seas of longhorn cattle being herded become a familiar sight. Cattle had grown wild since the Spanish brought livestock to New Spain. About five million longhorns, a cross between Spanish cattle and wild US cattle, roamed the cattle ranches of the prairie. They were bigger and hardier.

Tie a Cowboy Knot

Knots were very important to the cowboy. They were used to tie things together or to make a quick lariat to rope a cow or horse. The cowboy's knot had to be fast to tie and fast to untie. Popular cowboy knots were the Quick Release Knot (or Jerk Knot) and the Bowline Knot.

Materials

★ Length of rope

QUICK RELEASE

1. Make a loop in the rope and place it behind a post or rail with the loop to the right side and the ends of the rope to the left.

2. The rope to the left of the post that holds your horse—or whatever you need to tie up— is called the standing line. A few inches from the post, make another loop in the standing line.

3. Pass this second loop in front of the post and through the first loop. Pull the loose, bottom tail of the rope, called the working end, to tighten the first loop around the second loop.

4. Take the working end you just pulled and make a third loop a few inches down.

5. Pass this third loop through the second loop and pull on the standing line to tighten the knot.

6. The knot should hold if you tug on the standing line, but it will quickly release if you tug on the working end.

BOWLINE KNOT

7. Now look at the single Bowline Knot illustration. Can you tie this knot?

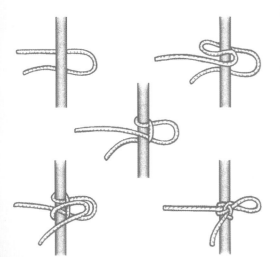

Called drovers at first, men of all races who led the drives became known simply as cowboys. For a time the cowboy became a symbol of Texas. A cowboy's life was a hard one. He worked long days in all kinds of weather. He faced stampedes and clouds of choking dust. But for many, life was to be lived in a saddle in the great outdoors. It only took about a dozen cowboys to handle 3,000 longhorns.

During the 1870s, cowboys drove millions of cattle from Texas across Indian and Oklahoma Territories to Abilene on the Chisholm Trail, perhaps the most famous of the cattle trails. The trail followed the old Shawnee Trail along San Antonio to Waco. Ther-e, the trail divided. The Chisholm Trail passed through Fort Worth before entering Indian Territory. The trail continued north, west of Oklahoma City until it reached Newton, and then Abilene in Kansas.

The cowboy became such a symbol of Texas and the West that it was immortalized in books and, later, movies. Rancher Larry Chittenden wrote a poem in 1890, "The Cowboys' Christmas Ball," inspired by a fire that burned down the Anson Star Hotel that year. The hotel had been the location of an annual Christmas dance. In 1934, the poem was set to music and sung at the first annual Cowboys' Christmas Ball in Anson.

The Great Storm

The Texas coast is like no other. At 367 miles long, it stretches from the wetlands at the Louisiana border to the southern tip where the Rio Grande empties into the Gulf of Mexico and Mexico begins. Yet the seven barrier islands—islands that run parallel to the mainland—and numerous bays actually add up to 3,300 miles of shoreline. Estuaries, wetlands, beaches, and cities line the shores of Texas. Many of the locations show their Spanish history with names like Laguna Madre, Padre Island, Corpus Christi, Matagorda Bay, and Bolivar Peninsula.

Tall ship *Elissa*, Galveston, Texas.
Library of Congress (LC-DIG-highsm-12683)

For many, the Texas Gulf Coast was the doorway into Texas. The Spanish first landed there in 1527. The French, British, and Americans explored Texas from the coast as well. And between 1835 and 1935, more than 200,000 immigrants came to the United States via Galveston, known as the Ellis Island of the West.

Exploring the Coast

When rumors reached the viceroy of New Spain, the Marqués de Cruillas, of English people on the islands in 1765, he asked Governors José de Escandón and Diego Ortiz Parrilla to investigate. They learned a lot about the area, such as how many long narrow barrier islands lined the coast, separated from the mainland by marshes or bodies of water about two leagues wide. While no British were found, the Spanish did see beaches littered with rigging and masts from ships. On Brazos Island, the remains of a 20-gun English ship was discovered. But the only inhabitants were the Native Americans of the area, such as the Malaguita.

Ortiz Parrilla turned in a map detailing his findings. While not totally accurate, it did show islands, rivers, bays, and where various bands of native people resided. Mention was made of great storms and flooding as well.

One location missing from Ortiz Parrilla's map was Galveston Island, which was curious because it was the first known location where Europeans landed. Within 20 years of Ortiz Parrilla's map, the two-mile-long island was colonized and named after Spanish governor and general Bernardo de Gálvez.

For hundreds of years, ships like the *Elissa* sailed in the Gulf waters. Built in Scotland, the *Elissa* was a tall three-masted ship with an iron hull and 19 sails. The ship's name came from a Roman poem, *The Aeneid*. The *Elissa* was 205 feet long and 99 feet, 9 inches at its tallest point.

The *Elissa* sailed the world for 90 years, carrying cargo to various ports. It was rescued first from a Greek scrap yard by the San Francisco Maritime Museum, and then from a salvage yard by the Galveston Historical Foundation in 1970. It was restored to its former glory, and today is the centerpiece to Galveston's Texas Seaport Museum.

Navigating ships around the barrier islands was tricky, and many ships landed at the bottom of the ocean instead. To keep ships from crashing or running aground, lighthouses were erected at various locations, including Matagorda Bay and Point Bolivar. The Point Bolivar lighthouse lit the way into Galveston Bay. The Port Isabel lighthouse, built by the United States in 1852, was 82 feet above sea level. The light from its 15 lamps and 21 reflectors could be seen for 16 miles.

In all, Texas had seven lighthouses. Today, that number is down to five, although with modern navigation only the Matagorda and Aransas Pass lighthouses are active. The biggest ports, Galveston and Corpus Christi, now use harbor lights. The others are maintained for historical interest and tourism.

Pirate Haven

As SHIPWRECKS were common and authorities were few along the Texas coast, it also attracted another type of visitor: pirates. Pirates, often from France or England, sailed the Gulf of Mexico looking to target Spanish galleons that carried treasure. Pirates found the barrier islands and sand dunes ideal for shielding ships from view.

Louis Michel Aury was a French pirate who sold his services to various governments. A quarrel with Bolivian leader Simón Bolívar led to Aury's joining the Mexican rebels in their revolt against Spain. In appreciation, they made him commissioner or leader of Galveston Island while his crew sailed the Gulf, searching for valuable cargo.

Another pirate, Jean Lafitte, secretly worked for the Spanish government. He convinced Aury of his loyalty to the Mexican rebellion. When Aury left the island to attend to business, Lafitte put his considerable charm and business

skills to converting the island's inhabitants. Aury's leadership had always been in turmoil, so it wasn't difficult. By September 1817, Jean Lafitte had assumed control of Galveston Island and a significant smuggling operation. Lafitte's base grew to include over 200 houses and hotels. Its headquarters was Maison Rouge, a two-story building painted red.

When looking at the history of pirates, it's sometimes hard to separate truth from legend. What is believed is that Jean Lafitte and his older brother, Pierre, had a French father and a Spanish mother. They may have spent at least some of their childhood in Española, a Spanish colony off the coast of South America, or the French Caribbean island of St. Domingue. Pierre set up a smuggling base near New Orleans.

Before taking over Galveston Island, Lafitte worked for the American government in the War of 1812 by supplying information and weapons to the Americans with the hope of being pardoned for his criminal activities. President Jackson even commended Lafitte for his courage. Actually, it's more likely that Lafitte played the United States and Spain against each other.

Pierre is sometimes credited with being the brains of the Lafitte brothers, but it was Jean Lafitte who sent merchant ships running away in fear and caused women to swoon. Martha Martin told of being on a sinking ship with her husband and family when they were rescued by Lafitte's crew. They were fed, and then Lafitte supplied a boat to take them home. He was known as the "Pirate of the Gulf" to some. He preferred "Governor of Houston."

His Galveston colony was home to about a thousand at its peak, but with the United States intent on shutting him down, he finally left for Central America in 1820. Before he left, he burned the town down, leaving behind rumors of buried treasure.

The Rich and Famous of Galveston

AFTER MEXICAN independence, Galveston began to be settled in earnest. Michel Menard and Samuel May Williams were among the earliest settlers. Mexican citizen Juan Seguin purchased 4,600 acres on Menard's behalf in 1836. Two years later, Menard House was built. The Greek revival home is the oldest home on the island. A year later, the city of Galveston was incorporated.

As the state's largest city and busiest port, Galveston drew the nation's elite as the third richest city per capita in the United States by the last half of the 1800s. The deepwater port stayed busy exporting 60 percent of the state's significant cotton crop. Approximately a thousand ships sailed in and out each year, plus regular railroad service carried cargo to and from the Galveston port. It was the first place in Texas to have electricity and telephones. The first post office, opera house, and golf course were also in Galveston.

Galveston drew a significant African American population too. In addition to being the home of Jack Johnson, the first African American heavyweight boxing champion of the world, many professionals came from Galveston. The Lone Star State Medical, Dental, and Pharmaceutical Association was founded in Galveston in 1886. This group of African American medical professionals was refused admission into the Texas Medical Association, so they formed their own, the second in the nation. Members included Monroe Alpheus Majors, the first African American physician west of the Mississippi River. Membership remained strong until the Texas Medical Association opened its doors to African Americans in 1955.

The Beach Hotel was a popular vacation destination due to the warm shallow waters on the beach nearby. Other visitors wintered in Galveston, but increasing numbers decided to make the booming seaport town of Galveston their permanent home.

James Moreau Brown was the youngest of 16 children in a New York family. He was apprenticed to a brick mason for a time, and came to Galveston while still in his 20s. Brown opened a hardware store and became very successful. He decided that he and his growing family needed a home that reflected that prosperity.

Building started on his Italianate villa in 1859. Two years later, the family moved into Ashton Villa. Ashton was a family name of Brown's wife, Rebecca. In all, the couple raised three boys and two girls. It was the girls who made the biggest impression. The middle child and first girl was Rebecca Ashton, named after her mother but going by Bettie. At a time when women of her social station didn't have professions, she was an artist who never married. She lived in Ashton Villa her entire life and was joined by her sister in 1896, when Mathilda divorced her husband and returned home with her three children.

Since 1970, Ashton Villa has been owned and operated by the Galveston Historical Association, which opens the house for public tours and special events.

While one of the small city's most famous homes is an Italianate villa and another is Greek revival style, Galveston is more known for its Victorian architecture. Downtown Galveston, specifically an area known as the Strand, showcases this ornate style. In 1900, the Strand was the Wall Street of the Southwest. Later in the 20th century, it became a showplace of Victorian architecture that sits on the US National Register of Historic Places

The Strand. Karen Gibson

as does the Romanesque Revival style Grand 1894 Opera House, where the rich watched the opera.

The home that best shows the Victorian influence is Bishop's Palace, designed by architect Nicholas Clayton. After the Civil War, attorney and Confederate colonel Walter Gresham brought his wife and children to Galveston. He was one of the founders of the

Gulf, Colorado and Santa Fe Railroad. He also served as a district attorney and later as a state representative.

The stone and steel Bishop's Palace was originally referred to as Gresham House, but it was later used by the Roman Catholic Church as the bishop's residence. The interior has marble columns, a mahogany staircase and fireplace, and bronze dragons.

The Great Storm

ONE DOWNSIDE to living on the Texas coast is the threat of hurricanes. During the summer storm season, early native residents moved inland. But the European settlers either didn't recognize the signs or couldn't move quickly enough to escape.

Tropical storms and hurricanes have hit the Texas coast many times. The second busiest port in 19th-century Texas was Indianola, founded in 1846 on Matagorda Bay. Twenty-nine years later, a two-day hurricane caused significant devastation to the community of 5,000. Efforts to rebuild started, but in 1886 another hurricane and fire wiped out Indianola.

In 1900, Galveston was no longer the largest city in Texas. Dallas, Houston, and San Antonio had surpassed it. Hurricanes weren't unknown in Galveston. In fact, one hurricane had damaged Lafitte's colony. But the people and the island always bounced back from storms. That is, until the Great Storm of 1900 struck the city of over 37,000 people.

The morning of September 8, 1900, dawned as a typical day in Galveston, warm and sunny.

Bishop's Palace, also known as Gresham's Castle. Library of Congress (LC-DIG-highsm-18754)

Children played in the surf and everyone went about their daily business. Only chief meteorologist Isaac Cline from the US Weather Station at 23rd and Market Street noticed the changes. The water around the island was rising faster than normal. Winds grew stronger, and the barometer dropped.

Knowing that danger was imminent, Cline jumped on his horse and warned people away from the beach. He told everyone within three blocks of the surf to move to higher ground. People didn't listen at first. Cline's belief that a safe place existed on the island was wrong; the city was only eight to nine feet above sea level at its highest point.

Cline sent updates to the Weather Center's office in Washington, DC, by telegraph until the lines went down mid-afternoon. There was nothing more he could do. He left for his strongly built house, which had attracted approximately 50 people in his absence.

As the day progressed, no doubt remained of the danger. The winds increased to an estimated 130 to 140 miles per hour, and the water continued to rise. The water from the bay and the ocean met at 15th Street. When it looked like second stories wouldn't be high enough, some climbed out to the roofs, only to be struck by flying debris.

People took shelter where they could—in the lighthouse stairwell, at homes, or in the

Bake a Sunshine Cake

Mrs. Gresham of Bishop's Palace was known for her Sunshine Cake. The recipe was published in the *Charity Ball Cookbook* on April 17, 1900, and is adapted here.

Adult supervision required

Ingredients for Cake
* ★ 10 egg whites
* ★ 1½ cups sugar
* ★ 5 egg yolks
* ★ 3 teaspoons of orange juice
* ★ Orange zest (grated orange peel)
* ★ 1 teaspoon cream of tartar
* ★ ¾ cup flour

1. Preheat oven to 325° F.

2. Beat the egg whites lightly.

3. Add sugar to the egg whites and beat until thick.

4. Separately, mix the egg yolks, orange juice, and orange zest.

5. Mix the two egg mixtures together.

6. Add cream of tartar to the flour, and then stir it into the egg mixture.

7. Pour into cake pan and bake for approximately an hour.

Ingredients for Icing
* ★ ¾ cup sugar
* ★ ¾ cup water
* ★ 1 egg white
* ★ Zest and juice of 1 lemon

1. Mix the sugar and water. Boil until the mixture thickens.

2. Beat the egg white and add it to the sugar mixture.

3. Add the juice and grated zest of one lemon.

4. Let icing stand until thick enough to put on cake.

ACTIVITY
Hurricane in a Bottle

Tornados are very destructive due to their high-speed, circular winds. Hurricanes are even more damaging because they occur over open water and can lead to storm surges, which raise sea levels and flood coastal cities.

Materials
★ 2 2-liter soda bottles
★ Water
★ 2 ounces vegetable oil
★ Drill and ¼-inch bit
★ Duct tape

Adult supervision required

1. Fill one of the 2-liter bottles with water.

2. Add two ounces of vegetable oil to the bottle.

3. Place the two bottle caps back to back and, with an adult's help, drill a ¼-inch hole through the center of both.

4. Screw both bottle caps back on to the bottles.

5. Tape the two bottles together at the bottle caps. Make sure the holes are lined up with the empty one on top and the filled one on bottom.

6. When the bottles are completely taped, turn them over so that the filled bottle is on top and gently start moving the bottles in a circular manner.

8. You should see a swirl in the center of the bottle as the water runs from top to bottom.

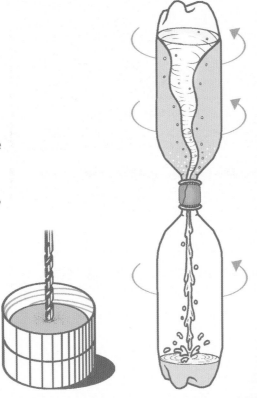

infirmary. Cline wrote in his memoir, "There was no island, just the ocean with houses standing out of the waves which rolled between them."

Storms surges covered the island. The 15½-foot main surge struck the south shore of the island at 7:30 PM. The water yanked houses from their foundations and slammed them into other houses. The weight of the tide caused buildings to collapse all over the island. The storm surge brought with it a wall of debris two stories high.

Night had fallen and all was dark. Only flashes of lightning provided brief illumination as the storm beat the island. Families thrown into the waves grasped onto anything they could to save their lives. The storm began to subside by midnight, but those who lived had to wait until the sun rose before they knew their circumstances. More than half of the people at the meteorologist's house lost their lives, including Cline's wife.

When the sun rose, it was to find a third of the city destroyed. Thousands of buildings were gone. Piles of debris covered neighbors, friends, and family. The death toll ranged from 6,000 to 8,000. The smell of decaying fish, animals, and humans soon overwhelmed the survivors. Some left Galveston, never to return.

Others got to work. There were so many bodies. At first, they tried to weigh down the bodies for burials at sea, but so many bodies came back that instead funeral pyres were built throughout the city to burn remains.

Perhaps saddest of all was what had happened at the St. Mary's Orphan Asylum at 69th Street and Seawall Boulevard. The Sisters of Charity had opened the first Catholic hospital in the state to care for the many immigrants entering Texas. Soon they opened an orphanage for those children who lost their parents in yellow fever epidemics.

The children and nuns first waited in the chapel, where they sang an old French hymn called "Queen of the Waves." French fishermen used to sing it as protection from storms. They sang:

Queen of the Waves, look forth across the ocean

The sand dunes between the orphanage and the beach collapsed as if the dunes were made of flour. Still the water kept rising. The nuns took the children to the highest part of the orphanage, the second floor of the girls' dormitory. The girls' dormitory was newer and stronger than the boys' dormitory. The singing continued.

See how the waters with tumultuous motion
Rise up and foam without a pause or rest.

The water began flooding the first floor. Not wanting children to wander off or be carried off into the ocean, each nun tied herself to several children with clothesline. A few older chil-

An opened passageway in the Galveston debris, looking north on 19th Street.
Library of Congress (LC-USZ62-123886)

dren made their way to the roof. They heard the boys' dormitory crash down, and again the nuns urged the children to sing.

Help, then sweet Queen, in our exceeding danger...

The singing stopped when the girls' building collapsed. Three boys survived, finding

Seawall along the beach in Galveston, Texas.
Library of Congress (LC-USW3-027868-E)

Storm" refers to. (Names weren't used for hurricanes until 1953.) It remains the worst natural disaster in terms of lives lost in recorded North American history—worse than the San Francisco earthquake or Hurricanes Katrina or Sandy.

The eyes of the world were on Galveston. They were helped by a disaster relief organization, the American Red Cross, founded by Clara Barton. At 78 years of age, Barton thought her days of providing care and aid were over, but she couldn't ignore the people of Galveston. She and a group from Washington, DC, arrived as soon as they could.

Property loss was estimated at $28 to $30 million. But people started to rebuild. Building a seawall was first on the list after cleanup. The 17-foot-high concrete wall trailed the Gulf for 3.3 miles. Afterward, the city leaders decided to raise the city. At the seawall, Galveston was raised 16 feet, and then gradually declined toward the bay side. Over 2,100 buildings were raised with jacks while sand was pumped under the buildings.

Streets were graded and paved. Homes and businesses were rebuilt. The streetcar rails were relaid. Rebuilding Galveston was paid for with bonds through property taxes and individuals. It was finally finished in 1928.

Before the rebuilding was finished, the seawall was tested with hurricanes in 1909 and

themselves in a tree in the water. The remaining 90 children and 10 nuns were killed.

Each year on September 8, the Sisters of Charity stop what they are doing to honor those who lost their lives in the Great Storm. At locations throughout the world, the Sisters of Charity sing "Queen of the Waves." And in Galveston, they lay a wreath and pray.

Even today, over a hundred years later, everyone in coastal Texas knows what the "Great

1915. Destruction was significantly reduced, and only eight people were killed in the 1915 storm. But city leaders were always looking at ways to protect Galveston. The seawall was extended in 1927 and again in 1963.

Residents celebrated in 1912 when a causeway connecting Galveston to the mainland was finished. People can now come to and leave Galveston Island in two ways, the causeway across the bay and a ferry to Point Bolivar.

While Galveston was rebuilding, Houston dug a ship channel. Soon, much of the commerce was being conducted in Houston. Galveston became a resort town. In the 1980s, the people of Galveston began to focus on the island city's culture and history with the result that more than 2,000 buildings are listed on the National Register of Historic Places. The Strand Historic District is a centerpiece, particularly at Christmas and Mardi Gras. At Christmas, Galveston presents Dickens on the Strand, where people dressed up in Victorian clothing sing carols. The Mardi Gras celebration pulls in half a million visitors a year.

Yet all the rebuilding and civic pride can't stop Mother Nature. The third largest hurricane of the 1900s, Hurricane Beulah, unleashed its fury on South Texas and North Mexico in 1967. Galveston was safe, but the hurricane led to tornados that caused 24 Texas counties to be declared disaster areas.

The Houston Ship Channel. Library of Congress (LC-DIG-highsm-13418)

Galveston wasn't as lucky when Hurricane Ike arrived on September 13, 2008, with a storm surge approaching 20 feet. But Galveston has proven itself a survivor. When devastation hits, it's time to pick up, go back to the drawing board, and rebuild.

Coastal Life

COASTAL LIFE isn't limited to humans; all types of creatures from alligators to birds live along the Texas coast. The weather and variety of habitats prove ideal for all types of life.

The open water is home to fish and mammals of all sizes and species. The American eel lives in the Gulf, and people riding on the ferries watch for the dolphins that like to swim in the warm waters. Various species of snappers and eastern oysters live near the reefs off the coast.

The brackish wetlands, a mixture of saltwater and fresh water, are home to various crabs, such as the hermit and fiddler crabs. The hermit crab is known for carrying around a gastropod shell that it can withdraw into. The shell helps protect the crab's soft abdomen. As the hermit crab grows, it must find bigger shells to accommodate its larger body.

Texas hermit crab. Karen Gibson

Kemp's ridley sea turtle nesting. National Park Service, Wikimedia Commons

What makes the fiddler crab unique is that it moves sideways instead of forward or backward. Males are easy to detect because their claws are different sizes, one large and one small. If a crab loses a claw, it will just grow back. Fiddler crabs like to burrow in the soft sand or mud of the salt marshes. There's plenty of food and places to hide.

American alligators can live in brackish (salty) water as well, but they prefer the shallow fresh water of swamps or bayous. At 6 to 14 feet long, the alligator is fast on land and water. Since it's carnivorous with sharp teeth, most people try to avoid them. The feeling is mutual—most alligators try to avoid people as well.

Texas alligators are most dangerous from March through May, which is the peak time for breeding and nesting. Alligators are every bit as protective of their young as many mammals. After birth, hatchlings are about nine inches long and will stay with their mother for about two years.

The American alligator was placed on the endangered species list in 1969, but removed in 1985 due to increased populations. It is now considered a protected game animal, and a permit is required to hunt them.

Pelicans and turtles also like the shallow water of the estuaries. One species of turtle, the Kemp's ridley sea turtle, uses Texas shores for nesting. Each year, female turtles come to one specific beach to dig a hole and deposit about a hundred eggs before returning to the sea.

If undisturbed, the eggs will hatch in 50 to 55 days with the half-dollar-sized baby turtles heading immediately to sea. If they are male, they will remain at sea their entire life. If female, they will start nesting between 10 and 15 years of age at the same beach where they were hatched. No one really knows how the turtles know what beach to come back to. Perhaps they attach to a chemical imprint or magnetic location.

Nesting sites are protected. The Rancho Nuevo beach in Mexico is the primary site for nesting, but a secondary site has been established at Padre Island National Seashore, the longest of the barrier islands.

The smallest of the sea turtles, the Kemp's ridley turtle, is also the most endangered. The turtles have many predators that feed on them or their eggs. Humans have long been a problem as well. For a long time, people harvested the eggs or killed the turtles for their meat, skin, or shells. These days, turtles are more in danger from eating floating trash or being caught by boat propellers or fishing nets.

One of the more dangerous creatures on Texas beaches and surf is the Portuguese man-of-war, often referred to as a jellyfish due to its transparent bubble. Although similar in

Grow an Artificial Reef

Coral reefs are important to ocean life, but they are disappearing due to environmental problems like human activity, water pollution, and climate change. In addition to supporting plant and animal life, coral reefs contain potential sources of medicines to treat a variety of conditions.

Some agencies and organizations are trying to help by creating artificial reefs. These man-made structures are best made from concrete or limestone.

Materials

★ Aquarium

★ Sand

★ Cinderblock or brick
(The best shapes are those that have arches or large holes in them.)

★ Water

★ Aquarium light

1. Add sand to the bottom of an aquarium.

2. Add the concrete block carefully to the middle of the aquarium.

3. Add enough water to cover the block by at least a couple of inches.

4. If you have an aquarium light, place it on top of the aquarium. Oceans receive a lot of sunlight.

5. After time, algae will form on the object. In the ocean, invertebrates like coral or barnacles also attach to the reef. All of this is food for plants and animals.

appearance, a man-of-war isn't actually a jellyfish; it's a siphonophore, an animal made up of a colony of organisms that work together. It's an interesting-looking creature, but the last thing you want to do is to come in contact with it. The man-of-war has tentacles armed with special cells called nematocysts, which can cause a quite painful sting if touched.

Many coastal or marine animals begin their lives in estuaries. Sometimes they need a little help, and that's where Texas wildlife officials, the Texas Marine Science Institute, and others lend a hand to prevent overfishing. For instance, limits are placed on certain fish. Meanwhile, fish hatcheries spawn and release various species to aid the natural reproduction. Within a 10-year period, over 1.1 billion red drum fry were released into estuaries.

The Texas Parks and Wildlife Department (TPWD) also manages the Texas Artificial Reef Program in the Gulf of Mexico. They take old ships, car bodies, concrete pipes, and petroleum platforms and sink them into the Gulf to develop new reef sites.

8

From Oil Boom to Space Age

On a warm June day in 1894, a contractor with American Well and Prospecting Company was drilling for water. The town of Corsicana, about 55 miles from Dallas, had contracted for three new water wells in order to increase business development in the town. Instead of water, the contractor hit oil at 1,027 feet—and lots of it.

It wasn't the first sighting of oil in Texas. Luis de Moscoso, a survivor of the DeSoto expedition, was forced ashore near Sabine Pass at the northern part of the coast in July 1543. He reported an oily substance floating on top of the water. The group of explorers used the sticky gunk to seal their boats.

Nacogdoches merchant Lyne Taliaferro Barret and partners in the Melrose Petroleum Company leased 279 acres in 1859 for the purposes of finding oil. The Civil War postponed more extensive oil exploration and development. Still, the first producing oil well drilled at 106 feet at Oil Springs produced 10 barrels a day. But low oil prices made the cost of development more than the oil was worth. Years later, Barret was able to further develop the field during an oil boom.

The Heywood #2 gusher received worldwide attention and put Beaumont, Texas, on the map. Library of Congress (LC-USZ62-4723)

But the Corsicana oil field was the first to show significant commercial potential. The first modern refinery in Texas opened at the field in 1898, and within two years the Corsicana oil field was producing 839,000 barrels of oil in a year.

The discovery and success of Corsicana prompted more oil exploration in Texas. By then, the Texas legislature had set rules for oil exploration and drilling to reduce the danger of fire and to protect groundwater and natural gas. And it was a good thing, too. Texas was about to experience a significant oil boom.

The upper Gulf Coast became a favorite place for exploration. The Gladys City Oil, Gas, and Manufacturing Company experienced failure after failure on Spindletop Hill in Beaumont. For eight years, they continued trying. Money would run out and new financing would have to be arranged. A particular problem was drilling through the sands of the salt dome. Finally, with new investors and a heavy rotary bit for drilling, they hit gold—black gold, that is—on January 10, 1901. The 100-foot geyser could be seen for miles and took nine days to cap. With the Spindletop oilfield producing 100,000 barrels of oil a day, the Texas economy was changed forever.

In the first three months of 1929, Texas produced over 69 million barrels of oil. Several refineries and a pipeline system were developed. Major oil companies were born: Texaco, Standard Oil, and Gulf Oil Corporation. Processing capacities grew. The Houston Ship Channel, opening the same year that World War I started, attracted oil refineries.

The state made money, too. In 1906, the first full year of taxation based on 1 percent of the value, Texas pocketed $101,403. By 1919, the state was clearing a million dollars from oil taxation. Ten years later, $6 million.

Oil exploration gradually expanded to the rest of Texas, even on land owned by the University of Texas. Both UT and Texas A&M received oil royalties for years. When the Santa Rita pump stopped producing, it was moved to the University of Texas campus.

Wherever oil was discovered, industrial development followed, particularly in manufacturing. A carbon black plant in Stephens County in 1923 gave birth to the petrochemical industry. Significant natural gas fields were found in the Panhandle as well.

Texas population increased significantly as people rushed in to take part in the Texas oil boom. The surge of people working in the oil industry caused tent cities to go up overnight. The boom carried over, affecting towns and cities as well.

The city of Dallas, incorporated in 1882, became the place to live. It had streetcars, railroads, and horseracing in addition to the best streets in the state. Ninety percent of Dallas

homes had running water by 1889. The Texas State Fair and horseracing became important attractions.

When World War II started, Texas began curtailed oil exploration and production due to a steel shortage, rationing, and railroad shutdown days. Texas was producing less than 60 percent of its oil potential. After the war, markets for oil and gas multiplied and most restrictions were removed.

The 1950s brought a surge of drilling, with the West Texas Permian Basin becoming the leading oil-producing area in the United States. Although the Texas oil industry was doing well, changing federal regulations and foreign oil made the Texas oil industry less profitable. When there was a revolution in Iran in 1978, the supply of foreign oil dropped. The oil shortages led to increased prices. The Texas oil industry had to invest in exploration and energy-saving technology in order to continue to be one of the world's leading crude oil producers.

The last oil and gas boom for Texas took place in the 1970s and '80s, but Texas remains the top oil-producing state in the United States and is one of the biggest in the world with 74 million barrels of oil produced in March 2013. In 2008, the industry brought in $9.9 billion to the state and employed 1.8 million people.

Today, some attention is being focused on the impact of drilling. Boiling Dome has been

Tank cars of the oil companies from the Gulf Coast and Texas fields. Library of Congress (LC-USE613-D-003203)

ACTIVITY
Clean Up Oil Spills

Oil spills are a big problem. When the BP oil spill occurred in the Gulf of Mexico in 2006, large amounts of ocean life were killed. The effects of that oil spill continue today.

Materials
★ Newspaper
★ Large plastic garbage bag
★ Large liquid measuring cup
★ 4 or more absorbents to test; examples include cotton, hair or fur (ask at a pet groomers or beauty salon), straw, corncobs or husks, polypropylene pads or shop towels (auto supply section of stores)
★ Dry measuring cup, 1-cup size
★ Paper or glass bowls, 12-oz size, 3 bowls for each absorbent you are testing
★ Pitcher of water
★ 1 gallon vegetable oil
★ Single-serving mesh micro-screen coffee filter to fit in liquid measuring cup
★ Timer
★ Liquid soap
★ Paper or graph paper to document results

1. Spread newspaper onto your work surface.

2. Open the garbage bag and set it close to the liquid measuring cup.

3. Prepare and test your absorbents one at a time. Cut each one into finger-tip-sized pieces so you can keep your workspace uncluttered.

4. Divide one of the absorbents into three piles of 1 cup each. Put each pile into a bowl.

5. Pour 3 cups of water into the liquid measuring cup. Slowly add 1 cup of oil. Note whether the water and oil separate or mix.

6. Pour 1 cup of an absorbent into the coffee filter. Slowly lower it into the water-oil mixture until it is completely submerged.

7. Start the timer. After 30 seconds, lift the filter and absorbent out of the liquid. Let it drain for 30 seconds.

8. Dump the absorbent into the plastic trash bag.

9. Record the remaining oil/water level.

10. Wash out the micro-screen filter with soap and water.

11. Repeat steps 6 through 10 with the next two cups of absorbent.

12. Repeat steps 4 through 11 with the other three absorbents you have chosen.

Which absorbents absorb the most of the oil-water mixture? The least?

the site of oil, gas, and sulfur wells since the 1920s. In 1983, a 250-diameter and 25-foot deep sinkhole appeared there, causing a roadway to collapse.

The Future in Technology

LUCKILY, TEXANS knew that a strong economy meant diversification. In addition to the cattle and oil industries, Texas has been a leader in electronics, medicine, and computers.

In Houston, one cardiac surgeon wanted to be first to perform a heart transplant, a process that had once been unthinkable. It had been attempted two other times, once in South Africa and then at Stanford University in California. The recipients lived 18 and 15 days, respectively.

Experimentation had taken time, but finally Denton Cooley, MD, at St. Luke's Hospital in Houston, was ready. His patient, 47-year-old accountant Everett Thomas, had a heart that had been severely damaged by rheumatic fever. On May 3, 1968, Dr. Cooley transplanted the heart of a 15-year-old girl who had died into Thomas. Thomas lived for 204 days, longer than anyone else had so far.

Less than four months later, rival Texas surgeon Michael E. DeBakey performed the first multi-organ transplant. He removed two kidneys, a heart, and a lung from one donor and inserted them into four different patients.

Heart transplants continue to improve, and now artificial hearts have been implanted as well. The introduction of antirejection medications in the 1980s improved life expectancy. According to the Organ Procurement and Transplantation Network over 5,000 heart transplants have been performed at 18 heart transplant centers in Texas.

Texas Instruments was an early electronics company started in 1930 by two physicists. They produced the first portable transistor radios and handheld calculators. Texas Instruments had early success with developing silicon transistors, integrated circuits, and semiconductor microprocessors. In 1971, Texas Instruments, along with Intel, became

Aerial view of an oil refinery next to the Gulf of Mexico near Houston. Library of Congress (LC-DIG-highsm-12335)

the first to develop microprocessor computer chips.

After discovering that oil exploration technology had military and other industrial applications, the company also did work in submarine detection and missile guidance. Since the late 1980s, Texas Instruments has focused its efforts on military electronics and artificial intelligence.

The Microelectronics and Computer Technology Corporation (MCC) was a group of technology companies who joined together in 1982 to combine the resources of top US technology companies with breakthrough technologies. When it was time to choose labs to develop and test products, it became a fierce competition among 57 cities. Economy, business, and quality-of-life issues were debated as well as access to universities. In the end, Austin was selected as the site for the technology research and development company. Almost 400 workers joined the Austin economy. Although MCC dissolved in 2000, Austin experienced a technology boom with top companies like Dell, IBM, and others deciding to base operations there.

Another way Texas expanded its interests was in the air. Texas has a long history in aviation. A German inventor from Fredericksburg may have beat the Wright brothers into the air by 40 years. Jacob Friedrich Brodbeck reportedly flew an airship in a field east of Luckenbach in 1865. The machine reportedly rose 12 feet and traveled 100 feet before it crashed.

After the success of the Wright Brothers, Slats Rodgers built the first plane in Texas in 1912. After he built it, he took it up in the air although he hadn't learned to fly yet. He later became the first licensed pilot in Texas, working as a flight instructor, barnstormer, and stunt pilot. When he couldn't make enough money from these enterprises, he took to smuggling moonshine from Mexico to Texas in his airplane during Prohibition.

Other famed aviators from Texas include Bessie Coleman, the first African American to earn a pilot's license, and millionaire Howard Hughes, who set a record when he flew around the world in 3 days, 19 hours, and 17 minutes. During Hughes's record-setting flight in 1938, he also cut Charles Lindbergh's Atlantic crossing time in half. Hughes, already a film producer, later became involved in the aeronautics industry as well.

In 1940, President Franklin Roosevelt signed a bill to create a naval air station in Corpus Christi. Its purpose was to train navy pilots, gunners, navigators, and others involved in naval flight operations. The Corpus Christi Naval Air Station later expanded to include the Naval Air Advanced Training Command and the precision flight team the Blue Angels for a time.

Space: The Final Frontier

WITH GAINS in technology and aviation, it's not surprising that space became the next venture for Texas. On July 29, 1958, President Dwight D. Eisenhower signed the National Aeronautics and Space Act to investigate space exploration. The act led to the creation of the National Aeronautics and Space Administration (NASA).

After the Soviet Union had success with launching satellites into space starting in 1957, the number one goal of NASA became manned space flight. President Kennedy vowed to have a man on the moon by the end of the 1960s. NASA planned on three phases to reach that goal.

Phase 1 was Project Mercury, in which one man would take flight up to three days. Phase 2 was Project Gemini. These would be two-man flights to develop docking and rendezvous methods. Phase 3 was Project Apollo: the lunar mission

Central to the success of the program was a manned spacecraft center where training and flight control would take place. The Manned Space Center opened in 1961, 30 miles south of Houston. With the ship channel, Houston had a good way to transport space vehicles to locations like Cape Canaveral. It assumed flight control responsibilities with the 1965 *Gemini 4* flight, which included the first American space walk.

The first group of American astronauts, the Mercury Seven, gave Texas new heroes to replace the cowboys and oilmen—astronauts. The accomplished pilots, and later scientists, underwent the ultimate testing and training for the ultimate trip—into space.

While astronauts were launched from Florida's Cape Canaveral and landed there and at other locations, the Manned Space Center was where the astronauts trained for space flight and where the space shuttle was developed. The center is also where Mission Control operates. Mission Control monitors everything about the flights. If they see a problem, they let the flight team know. If the flight team experiences a problem, then Mission Control puts all its resources to work to fix it. Mission Control

★ Looking to the Skies

The eyes of Texas have long looked to the skies. On May 5, 1939, the University of Texas established the Austin McDonald Observatory in the Davis Mountains of southwest Texas. Construction on the Hobby-Eberly telescope, one of the world's largest optical telescopes, began in 1994. The 433-inch (11-meter) mirror was constructed for spectroscopy, the decoding of light from stars and galaxies. This allows astronomers to study the properties of and learn more about black holes, other planets, and distant galaxies.

is such an integral part of space explorations that modern culture has readily adopted a phrase used during the *Apollo 13* space mission. The original phrase was "Houston, we've had a problem," but the 1995 movie about that mission changed it to "Houston, we have a problem."

Exhibit at the Space Center Houston. Karen Gibson

Twelve years after opening, the Manned Space Center was renamed the Lyndon B. Johnson Space Center. It's now referred to as the Johnson Space Center. As senator and later president, Johnson was an important part of the development of the space exploration program.

Located on 1,600 acres, the center also includes research and development and the management of space operations. More than 19,000 people work at the center, including 100 astronauts.

Space flight caught the interest and imagination of so many people that the Space Center Houston visitor center opened in 1993. The visitor center was designed by Walt Disney Imagineering. In addition to touring the space center, visitors age 14 and up can take the Level 9 tour, which includes seeing Mission Control and astronaut training.

Texas Politicians

IN ADDITION to his role in the space program, Lyndon B. Johnson was one of many important politicians to come out of Texas. In fact, Texans have held all levels of national offices. Three have even become presidents: Lyndon B. Johnson, George H. W. Bush, and George W. Bush. However, Texas was an adopted state for the two Bush presidents. Of the three, only Johnson was a native Texan.

Make a Rocket

Materials

★ Small plastic water bottle with pull nozzle tip
★ White vinegar
★ Baking soda
★ Tissue
★ String
★ Cardboard
★ Scissors
★ Masking tape

1. Screw off the nozzle cap from a plastic water bottle. Fill the bottle about ¼ to ⅓ full with vinegar.

2. Put a spoonful of baking soda into the center of a piece of tissue. Fold the edges up and twist. Tie it off with a piece of string.

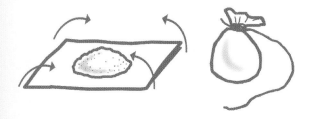

3. Holding on to the string, gently lower the baking soda–filled tissue into the bottle, *but do not let it touch the vinegar*. Screw the nozzle cap back on so that it holds the string and keeps the baking soda packet suspended above the vinegar. Set aside.

4. Cut a piece of cardboard roughly 8 inches by 12 inches. Fold it down the center lengthwise.

5. *OUTSIDE* (this is messy), prop the V-shaped cardboard up against a couple of bricks or a rock to make a launching pad. Use masking tap to hold it in place.

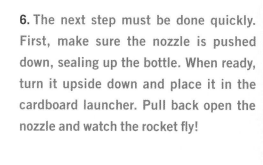

6. The next step must be done quickly. First, make sure the nozzle is pushed down, sealing up the bottle. When ready, turn it upside down and place it in the cardboard launcher. Pull back open the nozzle and watch the rocket fly!

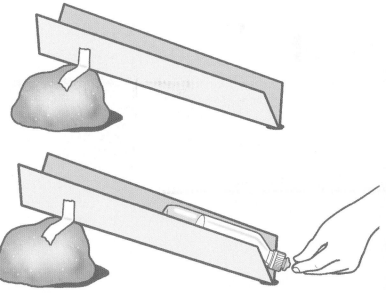

Born August 27, 1908, in the central Texas town of Stonewall, Johnson grew up in a rural area. His ancestor James Polk Johnson was the namesake for nearby Johnson City, which Lyndon Johnson would later call home.

After working his way through teacher's college, Johnson taught public school for a couple years before winning a seat in the House of Representatives. He took a break from political duty to serve as a lieutenant commander in the US Naval Reserve during World War II. He reported for active duty two days after the bombing of Pearl Harbor. He was awarded the Army Silver Star Medal for his service in the South Pacific.

After six terms in the House, Johnson was elected to the Senate in 1948. He served as both Minority Leader and Majority Leader during his tenure in the Senate.

In the late 1950s, the United States began looking at the 1960 election. Who would be the best leader for the nation? It came down to Richard Nixon and John F. Kennedy. Kennedy was different from previous candidates. He was younger, only 43. He was also Catholic, and the United States had never had a Catholic president. To broaden his appeal, Kennedy looked for a running mate who had the attributes he lacked—older, Protestant, and from the South. Lyndon B. Johnson fit the bill. The election was one of the closest in history. Kennedy and Johnson won with 49.7 percent of the popular vote and 303 electoral votes.

During a campaign trip to Dallas on November 22, 1963, Kennedy was assassinated. Later that day on the presidential airplane, Air Force One, Johnson was sworn in as president at 2:38 PM. He continued pushing Kennedy's civil rights legislation that focused on desegregation of schools and public places. It also removed unfair restrictions on African American voting rights. In 1964, the Civil Rights Act was passed. Later that year, Johnson won the presidential election with 61 percent of the vote.

Johnson continued to work on voting rights, Medicare, and against poverty. He also saw great progress in the space program that he had worked so hard for as senator and vice president. However, the latter part of his presidency was overshadowed by the war in Vietnam. Johnson retired to his Texas ranch after his term, dying of a heart attack in 1973.

Texas has always had colorful characters, and the field of politics was no exception. Once Texas was admitted to the Union, its many new southern residents influenced politics. Voting was limited to adult white males and wealthy slave owners dominated state offices. In the tradition of southern politics, Texas was strongly Democratic. In the early years, the Whigs were the Democrats' only competition.

Lyndon B. Johnson. Library of Congress (LC-USZ62-13036)

★ Kennedy Assassination

In 1963, President Kennedy was looking for re-election, only a year away. Despite the fact that his vice president was from Texas, Kennedy was not very popular in that state. Kennedy thought a campaign trip to Texas would help. He arrived in San Antonio on November 21 and, with Johnson, dedicated the US Air Force School of Aerospace Medicine. After attending a Houston dinner to support US Representative Albert Thomas, Kennedy flew to Fort Worth.

While Kennedy was attending a breakfast at the Fort Worth Chamber of Commerce on November 22, people were getting ready for his visit in Dallas. The *Dallas Morning News* ran a full-page advertisement titled "Welcome Mr. Kennedy to Dallas." The advertisement, paid for by three businessmen calling themselves the American Fact-Finding Committee, was really an anti-Kennedy ad.

Other people were very excited about the visit, lining the streets to get a glimpse of President Kennedy in his motorcade as he was transported to the Dallas Trade Mart, where he would have lunch with Dallas civic leaders and businessmen.

After a 13-minute flight to Dallas, President Kennedy and his wife, Jackie, sat in an open car behind Texas governor John B. Connally and his wife, Nellie. Vice President Johnson and his wife, Lady Bird, were seated in another car. The noise was deafening as people cheered and waved to the president. Nellie Connally turned around and said, "Mr. President, you can't say Dallas doesn't love you."

Seconds later, as the car turned off Main Street at Dealey Plaza, shots were fired. President Kennedy was hit in the neck and head. The first shot also hit Governor Connally in the chest. The car sped to Parkland Hospital, just minutes away. The president was pronounced dead at 1:00 PE.

Police arrested Lee Harvey Oswald later that afternoon at the Texas Theatre for the death of a policeman. The next day, charges included murdering the president after a rifle was found on the sixth floor of the Texas Book Depository, which looked down over Dealey Plaza. Oswald was an employee there.

Two days after Kennedy's death, Oswald was being transferred to a county jail when a nightclub owner named Jack Ruby shot him. Oswald died at the same hospital as Kennedy, Parkland, two hours later.

The assassination of President Kennedy has been the subject of much investigation and theory in the past 50 years. What really happened continues to be debated today.

John F. Kennedy motorcade, Dallas, November 22, 1963. Library of Congress (LC-USZ62-134844)

They were later joined by the American Party, better known as the Know-Nothings. The opinion of founding father Sam Houston carried a lot of weight in who was elected until the Civil War approached. Then, a growing number of leaders rejected him due to his attachment to Unionism. When Houston ran for governor as an Independent in 1857, he received his only defeat.

The Republican Party, the party of Lincoln, didn't receive any support until after the war when federal military officers decided that incumbents were obstructing Reconstruction and replaced them with Republicans. As the political parties evolved, changes slowly took place, and an increasing number of Texans became Republicans after 1950.

But before the turn of the century, local Democratic politicians had a lot of clout and they weren't afraid to use it. In Fort Bend County, a white political group known as the Jaybirds issued an ultimatum in 1888—African American politicians must leave the county within 10 hours. This led to the Jaybird-Woodpecker War. The Woodpeckers were politicians supported by the Republican and African American community. The dispute continued with violence at times. The next year, the so-called Battle of Richmond expelled the Woodpeckers from office, and the white-only Jaybirds dominated county politics for the next 70 years.

In other counties, people in power were able to coerce voters or fix votes to come out in certain ways. But things were slowly changing. Even among the Democrats, changes were taking place. In 1922, a group of Independent Democrats met in Dallas to oppose the Ku Klux Klan and candidates from that organization.

The first Democratic National Convention to be held in the South after the Civil War was in Houston on June 29, 1928. Unfortunately for Texas, the Democratic candidate for president was Al Smith, a Catholic, anti-Prohibition politician. Texans as a whole were against Smith, and many campaigned against his nomination. When that didn't work, they turned their support to Herbert Hoover, giving the Republican candidate a majority in the state. It was the first time a Republican had carried Texas. Today, the Republican Party is strong in Texas.

The number of Hispanic politicians in Texas or from Texas continues to grow. Some notable politicians include Henry Cisneros, the first American-born Latino mayor of a major city (San Antonio) and Alberto Gonzales, the first Latino attorney general to the United States.

Women in Texas Politics

WHEN TEXAS became a state, women had few political rights, but they were allowed to own property regardless of whether they were married.

As in the rest of the United States, Texas women began voting in 1920 after the 19th Amendment passed. But before and after the passage of the 19th Amendment, Texas women were mainly outsiders to the world of politics. The main doorway into politics was through issues and causes. Many women held strong opinions about temperance, or restricting alcohol, for example. Later, labor laws affecting both children and women were big issues in Texas. Interest in health and safety at the workplace extended into municipal government—cleaner water, sanitation, and parks became political issues.

School reform issues were important as well, and school boards were some of the first elections that women won. Two women won seats for the Dallas school board in 1908; in San Antonio, three were elected in 1913.

Suffrage was also an issue that women had strong opinions about, both for and against. Pauline Wells began working against suffrage because she said it "identified with feminism, sex antagonism, socialism, anarchy, and Mormonism."

Regardless, many women in Texas did campaign for the right to vote. Texas actually began to allow women to vote in primary elections in 1918. Along with approximately 386,000 other women, Hortense Sparks Ward registered to vote in 1918. The first woman admitted to the Texas bar, she had already been a lawyer for eight years when she was allowed to cast her first vote.

Jane McCallum and other women like her had become active in the suffrage movement back in 1896. Once the 19th Amendment passed, McCallum worked for political reform as part of the Women's Joint Legislative Council. Commonly called the Petticoat Lobby, the group worked effectively on prison reform and ending child labor as well as improving health and education. McCallum was appointed secretary of state and served for two terms under two governors.

However, Ward, McCallum, and the Petticoat Lobby campaigned strongly against the first woman governor, Miriam A. Ferguson, better known as Ma Ferguson. Her husband, James Ferguson, had served as governor previously, but was impeached on various charges including misappropriation of funds. It was believed that although it was his wife who was running, it was really he who was making the decisions. Still, she was elected in 1924.

In Ma Ferguson's first term as governor, the Fergusons were accused of accepting bribes. She also pardoned an average of 100 convicts a month. When she ran for re-election in 1926, she was defeated by Daniel J. Moody with the help of the Petticoat Lobby. She was re-elected in 1932 and served an uneventful term.

Other than Ma Ferguson, women held few offices for many years. In 1922 Edith Wilmans became the first woman elected to the state legislature as a representative. The first female state senator was Margie Neal, who was elected in 1926 and served four terms. She was the only female senator in Texas for 50 years, however. Although it was difficult for women to get elected, they continued to work behind the scenes on political issues and rights for women.

The 1960s brought another woman to state government: Frances Farenthold. A state representative, Farenthold also ran for governor, losing in the Democratic primary by a narrow margin. By the late 1970s, Texas began electing women mayors in the larger cities. Kay Bailey Hutchison was elected to the US Senate as the first female Republican senator.

African American women in politics have had a more difficult struggle, as they had to fight against both racism and sexism. When Christia Adair was elected to the Harris County Democratic Executive Committee in 1966, the state convention refused to seat her. African American women worked with the National Association for the Advancement of Colored People (NAACP) and political committees to fight this kind of discrimination.

History was made when Barbara Jordan was elected to the state senate in 1966. She was the first African American since Reconstruction to hold that office, and the first African American woman. At the time of her election, she was the only woman and only African American in the state senate. She later became the first woman from Texas to be elected to Congress (Lera M. Thomas finished her deceased husband's unexpired term in 1966–67) and the first African American woman elected from the South. She served three terms. In 1976, Jordan gave the keynote address at the Democratic National Convention. She was asked to do it again in 1992.

Barbara Jordan was the youngest of three daughters and grew up in Houston. After graduating from Texas Southern University, she attended Boston University and received her law degree. In 1959, she passed the bar exams in both Massachusetts and Texas. She returned to Houston to open a law practice in her parents' home until she raised the funds to open her own office. Her entry into politics started with registering African Americans to vote. From there, her political career was born. She gained the respect of the 30 white men she worked with in the legislature and Lyndon Johnson as well.

Another Texas woman gave the keynote address at the 1988 Democratic National Convention—Ann Richards, who served as state treasurer for two terms. Two years later, she was elected governor in a fierce political contest.

Richards was born in Lacy-Lakeview, Texas. In high school, she was a member of the debate team and was declared state debate champion as a senior. After her marriage to David Richards, she taught government to junior high students in Austin while her husband attended law school. Richards first became involved in local politics as Travis County commissioner. In 1982, she successfully ran for state treasurer, the first woman to win a state office since Ma Ferguson.

Ann Richards was an outspoken and active governor. During her term, she initiated prison reform, school funding, and signed the Texas Financial Responsibility Law. She was defeated for re-election in 1994 by George W. Bush. Upon leaving office, she said, "I did not want my tombstone to read, 'She kept a really clean house.' I think I'd like them to remember me by saying, 'She opened government to everyone.'"

Another outspoken woman making a name for herself in Texas politics is Wendy Davis, an attorney elected to the Texas senate in 2008. She received national attention in June 2013 when she staged an 11-hour filibuster. She ran for governor in 2014.

Barbara Jordan at the 1976 Democratic National Convention. Library of Congress (LC-2002712192)

9

The American Southwest

T he image of the cowboy, the oilman, or the astronaut as representative of Texas doesn't give the full picture, because Texas is also a land of many cultures. The Institute of Texan Cultures states that Texas is made up of people from a hundred different countries, and each has put its mark on Texas.

Early colonization and being next-door-neighbor to Mexico led to a strong Latino influence. Texas would not be Texas without its Latino culture. People with a Latino background go by many names: Hispanic, la Raza, or Chicano. Sometimes their country of origin is used, as in

A roundup (for tourists) of longhorn cattle in the Stockyards, Fort Worth.

Mexican American. Unique to Texas is the word "Tejano," a Texan of Mexican descent.

Latino Influences

THE UNIQUE combination of Texas and Mexico has given rise to the term "Tex-Mex." Tex-Mex may be used to describe something with both Texan and Mexican influences, such as music or design. Perhaps the most common use of Tex-Mex is related to food.

Tex-Mex food is an often spicy combination of Spanish, Mexican, and Native American cuisine. Tortillas, either corn or flour, are used to wrap seasoned meat with chiles, cheese, beans, and sometimes other vegetables. Tacos, burritos, and enchiladas are all Tex-Mex foods. Corn is an important ingredient, whether making tortillas or the masa for tamales. Tamales are seasoned meat wrapped in a corn dough and steamed in corn husks. Traditionally, tamales were made for special occasions like Christmas, but now they are available any time.

For Texas, Latino culture also means lots of festivals, both locally and statewide. The three largest are Cinco de Mayo, Fiestas Patrias, and Dia de los Muertos.

Cinco de Mayo, meaning the Fifth of May, is a fiesta time with parades and dancing to mariachi music. It recognizes Mexico's victory against France in the Battle of Puebla on May 5, 1862. This holiday is bigger in the United States than in Mexico and has become a time to celebrate everything Latino culture has given us.

Cinco de Mayo is sometimes mistaken for Mexico's Independence Day, but that is actually September 16, when Father Miguel Hidalgo gave the cry for freedom from Spanish colonialism in 1810. People celebrate Mexico's independence from Spain with Diez y Seis de Septiembre (September 16), also known as Fiestas Patrias.

Fiestas Patrias was first celebrated in Texas in 1820 with music, dances, special costumes, and food. In the 20th century, San Antonio expanded it to a three-day celebration at the county fairgrounds. Parade participants, carrying the colors of both Mexico and the United States, include marching bands, dignitaries, and floats with famous people from Mexico represented. Afterward, Mexico's Declaration of Independence is read, followed by a 21-gun salute. Games, historical plays, food, and dancing follows, and on the final night, festivities are closed with a rousing fireworks show. San Antonio continues the three-day festival today in the downtown Market Square.

As time went on, Fiestas Patrias became an event in other Texas cities that started their own traditions. San Angelo's includes sports competitions, and in Houston, you can see

Make a Fiesta Flambeau Float

Another popular festival held in Texas is Fiesta Flambeau, the Battle of Flowers. Also known as Fiesta San Antonio, the annual springtime parade and festival is held in San Antonio to honor the battles at the Alamo and San Jacinto. Many parades include throwing flowers at each other, and many of the floats are also decorated with live and fake flowers.

PAPER FLOWERS

Materials

★ Colored tissue paper
★ Easy-to-bend, thin wire (like pipe cleaners from a craft store)

1. Lay a few sheets of tissue paper neatly on top of each other, making sure the edges and creases match.

2. Fold the stack of sheets accordion-style with each fold about an inch wide.

3. Wrap a wire around the center of the folded paper flowers. Wrap until the hold on the paper is secure. Twist the ends of the wire together.

4. Staple the wire to the tissue paper. Use the excess wire to make a stem.

5. Gently spread the folded paper open to make a round flower shape.

DECORATE YOUR FLOAT

Materials

★ Conveyance with wheels (wagon, stroller, bicycle, golf cart)
★ Brightly colored paper, such as butcher paper, craft paper, or tissue paper
★ Crepe paper
★ Ribbons
★ Other decorative items suitable for a float

1. Cover your wheeled float in a sheet or with paper so that its original shape isn't obvious.

2. Make a skirt with the crepe paper to go around the float.

3. Decorate the float with paper, glitter, and flowers.

native dances and costumes from different regions in Mexico. Mexican folklore and music are highlighted in the Port Arthur celebrations. In Austin, Tejano musicians play to crowds at the Fiesta Gardens in a six-day festival.

No doubt, the importance of Fiestas Patrias is why the launch of the festival is also the beginning of National Hispanic American Heritage month, from September 15 to October 15.

The third major Latino festival celebrated in Texas is Dia de los Muertos, or Day of the Dead, celebrated on November 1. The day is used to honor those who have died. Although Dia de los Muertos occurs the day after Halloween, it isn't about having fun with scary characters, but is a celebration of the circle of life. Traditionally, it was believed to be the time that souls return to Earth. Altars are set up in homes and at cemeteries, and it's common to see food or drink offerings left at graves.

For the living there is food as well. Pan de muerto or Day of the Dead bread comes in many shapes and varieties. Candy and cookie skulls are consumed as well. Parades are also held for Dia de los Muertos, but these floats are decorated with skeletons. Dressed in black, people may paint their face in black and white to look like a skeleton or they may dress up as a famous person who has died, such as Mexican artist Frida Kahlo or even Elvis Presley. A procession is held where the "dead" march, followed by a festival atmosphere of lively music and food.

★ Institute of Texan Cultures

The Institute of Texan Cultures was born in San Antonio at the 1968 World's Fair. It has evolved to a football field–sized building that recognizes, educates, and celebrates the many cultures of Texas from the last 30,000 years. In addition to exhibits and interpretive areas, the Institute of Texas Cultures is also a research facility, where writers and educators look through the extensive holdings and collections. Exhibits include such diverse materials as musical instruments, barbed wire, and arrow points. Behind the building is the Back 40, where visitors can look at 19th-century Texas to see the two-pens-and-a-dogtrot log home and barns where farmers worked. Visitors can also see how early residents used a windmill to power irrigation and the one-room schoolhouse attended by children.

Tejano Civil Rights

ALTHOUGH PEOPLE with a Mexican heritage played an important part in the history of Texas, Latino citizens often experience discrimination. Businesses once posted signs in windows stating NO MEXICANS ALLOWED. Instead of letting courts decide disputes, white vigilantes took the law into their own hands and lynched Tejanos.

Teacher, feminist, activist, and journalist Jovita Idar, a third-generation Tejano, lived in the border town of Laredo. She wrote about injustices for her family newspaper, *La Crónica*. In 1911, she and her family organized the first Mexican American civil rights conference in Texas, the Congreso Mexicanista.

Other civil rights conferences were held in other parts of Texas. Various chapters joined together and became the League of United Latin American Citizens (LULAC) in 1929. Fifty years later, Houston hosted the National Chicana Conference, the first national assembly of Mexican American feminists in the United States. Both racism and sexism were discussed.

Like African Americans, Tejanos weren't allowed to attend white-only public schools, which were supported by taxes. Idar's students often came to school hungry, and there was no money for books, equipment, or even heat for the classrooms. Until integration could be achieved, Idar opened free kindergartens and taught Latino children in English and Spanish.

Fifty years later, in 1968, students from Edgewood High School in San Antonio were still fighting the same fight. With a large Latino student population, Edgewood High School lacked books, supplies, and qualified teachers. Over 400 students staged a walkout, marching to the San Antonio district administration office. Parents filed suit for Latino students throughout the state. The federal district court ruled that the Texas system for financing

 ## The Texas Muse

Another activist and feminist was poet Sara Estela Ramírez. Although she was born in Mexico, she quickly adopted Laredo as her home after she moved there at age 17. In addition to writing poetry, Ramírez also supported the progressive political party Partido Liberal Mexicano. Jovita Idar referred to Ramírez as La Musa Texana or the Texas Muse on the poet's death in 1910 at age 29.

 ## Border Control

Illegal immigration has long been an issue in Texas. Ever since the United States established the Border Patrol in 1924, many people have crossed the Rio Grande in search of a better life. There are an estimated 3.5 million legal immigrants and another 1,740,000 undocumented workers in Texas, with the largest number from Mexico. Illegal immigration is an ongoing and controversial issue both in the state and in the United States.

schools was unfair to poor students and school districts with low property taxes. It was ruled unconstitutional.

Five years later, Governor Dolph Briscoe signed the Bilingual Education and Training Act, requiring bilingual education for any school with 20 or more children with limited English. It still took several years before bilingual instruction became common.

The Sounds of Texas

YOU MIGHT be able to guess that Latino music is big in Texas—not just salsa, but also Tejano music. Tejano music is a blend of American and Mexican music. Songs are sometimes sung in English and sometimes in Spanish. This uniquely Texan music originates in South Texas and was made popular by 1990s singing sensation Selena.

Although Selena grew up speaking English, she learned to speak Spanish so that she could sing songs in either language. She was the first musical artist to release a Tejano record that reached gold (meaning it sold more than 500,000 copies) and she won a Grammy in 1993 for Best Mexican-American Album. Two years later, just short of her 24th birthday, Selena was murdered by the head of her fan club.

Latino-influenced music is far from the only music that resonates with Texans. Rock 'n' roll, blues, gospel, jazz, and country music have significant followings as well. In addition to Tejano music, another form of music created in Texas is western or Texas swing. Fiddle player Bob Wills is generally credited with creating swing music, a style that uses infusions of jazz in country music. He and his group, the Texas Playboys, were popular in the 1930s and '40s.

Country music has been around Texas for some time and has launched countless careers. But often when people think of country music, Willie Nelson comes to mind. In the 1970s, Nelson began holding an annual country music festival in Forth Worth, Texas. Willie Nelson's 4th of July Picnic became a tradition with country music stars like Texan Waylon Jennings, Jimmy Buffet, and the Charlie Daniels Band performing. The Pointer Sisters, Neil Young, and Los Lonely Boys have also played at the festival.

Blind Lemon Jefferson is considered to be the founder of Texas blues. His records from the 1920s were among the first blues recordings to be commercially successful.

Texas blues artists like Jefferson influenced others in blues and rock 'n' roll, like brothers Johnny and Edgar Winter. Stevie Ray Vaughn was another influential blues and rock musician. The four-time Grammy award–winning guitarist was at the height of his fame when he died in a helicopter crash in 1990.

When rock 'n' roll first began, Texas was at the forefront with artists like Buddy Holly and Roy Orbison. Holly, from Lubbock, achieved phenomenal success with "That'll Be the Day," "Peggy Sue," "Oh Boy!" and "Not Fade Away." His influence was felt by many popular musicians, and he was among the first group of inductees into the Rock and Roll Hall of Fame.

Holly's career was cut short in a 1959 plane crash. He died along with fellow Texan J. P. Richardson, known as the Big Bopper, and California teenager Ritchie Valens.

Although Roy Orbison, born in Vernon, also began making music in the 1950s, his name didn't become well known until his 1960 recording, "Only the Lonely," a song he had written hoping to attract the attention of Elvis Presley or the Everly Brothers. It was the first of many hits in his 30-year music career. His first group was a country group, the Wink Westerners after his high school, Wink High School. His next group was a rock band, the Teen Kings, who performed "Ooby Dooby," their first hit.

Janis Joplin became a musical icon known for her powerful bluesy voice. Her appearance at the Monterey Pop Festival, singing the blues song "Ball and Chain," was a sensation. ("Ball and Chain" was originally recorded by another Texan, Big Mama Thornton.) Born along the coast in Port Arthur and dying in 1969, Joplin became one of the most famous female voices in rock 'n' roll.

The most popular Texas rock group in the 1970s and '80s was ZZ Top, who play guitar-driven Southern rock. The three-member group was inducted into the Rock and Roll Hall of Fame in 2004. And Texas's contribution to music continues. When the television show *American Idol* debuted in 2002, the first winner was Fort Worth singer Kelly Clarkson.

Texas continues to be a prime music location for both musicians and fans. Austin has earned a reputation as the "Live Music Capital of the World." Major musical stars have performed for the Austin City Limits and South by Southwest music festivals as well as other major festivals sponsored in the city.

Sports

STARTING WITH Pee Wee football and soccer, the competitive spirit that drives Texans to be first and best comes in handy in athletics. Eleven professional sports teams are based in

Roy Orbison mural in Wink, Texas, where he lived as a young man. Library of Congress (LC-DIG-highsm-12282)

★ Other Popular Texas Musicians and Groups

Bowling for Soup	Lead Belly	Kenny Rogers
Edie Brickell	Lyle Lovett	Jessica Simpson
T-Bone Burnett	Meat Loaf	Boz Skaggs
Freddie Fender	Johnny Nash	J. D. Souther
Don Henley	Michael Nesmith	Steve Miller Band
George Jones	Billy Preston	Stephen Stills
Scott Joplin	Ray Price	Sylvester "Sly" Stone
Kris Kristofferson	Tex Ritter	George Strait

Create a Zydeco Band

Zydeco is another type of music you hear in Texas. It's a type of folk music that originated among Creole and African Americans in the South in the late 1800s. Zydeco originated with poor people who didn't have the money to buy musical instruments, so they made instruments out of items they had around the house.

Recruit friends and classmates for a zydeco band. Look around your house for items to make music with. Once you have several "instruments" for your band, play some music!

Materials

★ Scrub board or washboards
  (used for washing clothes)
★ Shakers (such as uncooked beans in
  plastic Easter eggs)
★ Rattles (such as assorted buttons and
  beads strung on yarn)
★ Bells (such as jingle bells tied on either
  end of an empty paper towel roll)
★ Spoons

HOW TO PLAY SPOONS

1. Hold 2 spoons with the bowls of the spoons back to back.

2. Hold the spoons with your dominant hand (the one you write with), placing your index or second finger between the spoon handles.

3. Hit your spoons against your palm or thigh.

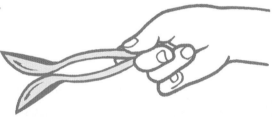

Texas, including two soccer teams and a hockey team, the Dallas Stars.

For students in high school and college, it's evident that three main sports dominate in Texas: baseball, basketball, and football. Baseball was introduced by northern soldiers during Reconstruction. For a time in the late 19th century, all the large cities had leagues. In modern times, Texas has two teams, the Houston Astros and the Texas Rangers (in Arlington). Both have made it to the World Series but never won a championship.

The same can't be said for basketball. Most recently, the Dallas Mavericks won their first championship against the Miami Heat in 2011. They are the youngest of the Texas NBA teams. The Houston Rockets won back-to-back championships in the mid-1990s, thanks largely to Hakeem Olajuwon, a power player who was nicknamed "Hakeem the Dream."

But the San Antonio Spurs top them all with four NBA titles. Joining the NBA in 1976, the San Antonio Spurs were a moderate success, winning divisional titles and qualifying for playoffs. The powerful combination of two players—center David Robinson and forward Tim Duncan—helped push the Spurs to their first NBA championship title in 1999. In 2003, the Spurs did it again, and David Robinson decided it was time to retire. But the Spurs had recruited a teenager from France, Tony Parker.

The Spurs won three more titles—2004, 2007, and 2014. The San Antonio Spurs are fourth in the league in the number of titles won.

The Houston Oilers were the first Texas football team, forming in 1960. But in 1997 the owner decided to move his team to Tennessee. Houston worked for years to get an NFL team back in the city, even building the NFL's first retractable-roof stadium. Both Reliant Stadium and the Houston Texans debuted in the 2002–2003 season.

The NFL's 13th franchise was awarded to Dallas at the beginning of 1960. The owners and general manager were too late for the college draft, but they knew who they wanted as coach: Tom Landry.

Tom Landry is a Texas institution. A product of Texas, he played for the University of Texas before taking a break to join the US Army Air Corps as a copilot and gunner of B-17 bombers during World War II. After flying 30 missions over Germany, he returned to the University of Texas to complete college. He played as a defensive back for the New York Giants. He exchanged playing for coaching, and used his analytical skills as defensive coordinator for the Giants. That is, until Texas came calling.

As soon as Landry accepted the job, he and the general manager did their best to assemble a team from the other 12 teams. The rule was that each team was allowed to choose their top

 ## The Super Bowl

The football championship game wasn't called the Super Bowl until the 1966–1967 season after the National Football League (NFL) and American Football League (AFL) decided to merge. In the first game, the Green Bay Packers defeated the Kansas City Chiefs.

Cowboys Stadium in Arlington. Library of Congress (LC-DIG-highsm-18733)

★ Dr Pepper Is a Texan

When pharmacist Charles Alderton wasn't filling prescriptions at Morrison's Old Corner Drug in Waco in 1885, he liked experimenting with soft drinks. The combination most popular with customers was named Dr Pepper by Wade Morrison, owner of the drug store. The company that makes Dr Pepper incorporated in 1923 and is now based in Plano, Texas. But the Dr Pepper Museum is still in Waco, and over a million people have visited the soft drink memorabilia there.

San Antonio. Library of Congress (LC-HS503-371)

25. Dallas got to pick from what was left. Their team name became the Cowboys. The team of veteran players and free agents didn't win one game that first season.

It's often joked that the first coach of the Dallas Cowboys never smiled. Landry, a disciplined man, continued to work on assembling and training a decent football team. After six seasons, it started to pay off. In 1966, the Dallas Cowboys won the Eastern Conference title, but lost to the Green Bay Packers at home by a touchdown. In 1967, the Cowboys lost to the Packers again, but this time by only four points. The location was the Packers turf in Wisconsin, where the freezing weather and ice led to everyone calling the game the Ice Bowl.

Things would only get better for the Cowboys in the 1970s because Landry found a quarterback—Roger Staubach—as disciplined about football as he was, and the Cowboys won their first Super Bowl in 1971. The Dallas Cowboys set records by reaching the playoffs eight years in a row. Their popularity led to all types of nicknames, from America's Team to God's Team.

In the 1980s, they broke their record of consecutive winning seasons when they hit 20, the most in professional football, and trailing only behind the New York Yankees (baseball) and Montreal Canadians (hockey) for all professional sports.

A change in owners led to a controversial change when Landry was fired. Players like Staubach retired, but new talent like Troy Aikman, Emmitt Smith, and Michael Irvin helped the Cowboys win back-to-back Super Bowls in 1992 and 1993.

With five Super Bowl wins, the Dallas Cowboys are tied for second with the San Francisco 49ers (the Pittsburg Steelers are first). While the Dallas Cowboys aren't winners every year, they are one of the best-known professional football teams in the United States.

Texas Tourism

TEXAS HAS long been a tourist destination. The commercial buffalo hunts and hot water spas in San Antonio were the must-see in the 19th century. By 1950, tourism was the fifth largest industry in the state.

Texas is also always in the top 10 lists of states visited by people from outside the United States. For domestic travel, Texas ranks only behind California and Florida. In 2010, Texas had almost 7.5 million visitors to its state parks and recreation areas. The revenue generated put Texas third behind Michigan and Indiana.

The size of Texas allows visitors to see beaches, forests, and deserts as well as canyons, caves, lakes, and hill country.

San Antonio is a popular tourist destination, offering the Alamo, the Mission Trail, and the

San Antonio Riverwalk.
Karen Gibson

Build a Bat House

Why build a bat house? Did you know that a single bat can consume a thousand mosquitoes an hour? Bat houses come in all shapes and sizes.

Adult supervision required

Materials

★ Hammer
★ Nails
★ Saw
★ Caulk
★ Adult helper

1. With an adult's help, cut or have the following wood precut:

★ 3 pieces of 1-inch × 8-inch board that are 22 inches long
★ 1 piece 1-inch × 8-inch board 17¼ inches long
★ 2 pieces 1-inch × 8-inch board 13 inches long
★ 1 piece 1-inch × 8-inch board 11 inches long
★ 1 piece 1-inch × 10-inch board 10 inches long

2. Measure 17¼ inches on one side of two of the 22-inch pieces. Cut the boards at an angle as shown. These two boards will be the sides of the house.

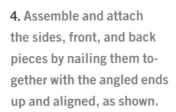

22″   17¼″

3. Cut a 33-degree edge on the top of the 17¼-inch board and the remaining 22-inch board. The 17¼-inch board will be the front of the house and the 22-inch board will be the back of the house.

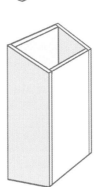

4. Assemble and attach the sides, front, and back pieces by nailing them together with the angled ends up and aligned, as shown.

5. Cut 33-degree edges on the tops of the 11-inch board and the two 13-inch boards. These will be the partitions inside the house.

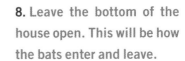

6. Insert the partitions, sliding them into box until the angled top edges align. Evenly space the partitions and nail them into place.

7. Place the 10 × 10 inch board on top of the angled section so that it lies flush with the tall back of the bat house and overhangs the shorter front. Nail the roof in place.

8. Leave the bottom of the house open. This will be how the bats enter and leave.

9. Caulk the exterior at the seams.

The most important thing is the location of the bat house. Bat houses placed in trees don't work as well as those on the sides of house or on poles. The location should receive at least 10 hours of sunlight a day, and 6 of those hours should be direct sunlight. For temperatures, bats like 80 to 100° F best.

Riverwalk. Shops and restaurants border the San Antonio River as it winds through town. Visitors can walk or take a leisurely boat ride. And in December, festive luminarias light the way.

Not far away is the state capitol in Austin. It is home to the largest capitol building in the United States, topping the US Capitol by seven feet. Nearby is the largest colony of Mexican free-tailed bats. They roost at the Congress Av-enue Bridge south of the Capitol. And music is always drawing crowds to Austin.

Tourists also come to sunny Texas to enjoy the miles of beaches. Padre Island, one of the many barrier islands along the Texas coast, is the longest with over 70 miles of beaches. It's a prime spring break and winter location. Galveston has the added benefit of intriguing history and is closest to Houston's Johnson Space Center.

LEFT: **Texas Capitol dome, Austin.**
Library of Congress (LC-DIG-highsm-12277)

ABOVE: **Texas beach.** Karen Gibson

The Road to Texas

When frontiersman Davy Crockett decided he had had enough of politics, he told people "they might all go to hell, and I would go to Texas." And that's exactly what he did. Through the years, millions of people have followed in his footsteps, and today you might see bumper stickers on cars that say, "Gone to Texas" or "GTT." Since 2000, one million people have migrated to Texas. They say enough to life somewhere else, and start anew in Texas.

Life isn't easier in Texas. From its earliest days, people have carved out homes with blood and sweat. Some fought against the terrain; others fought against wildlife or humans. Early settlers might have been drawn to the idea of cheap land, while others just wanted to escape the law.

People sometimes dealt with the lawless by shooting first and asking questions later.

Texas embraces diversity—ethnic, cultural, and even geographic diversity. It's a beautiful land with each region offering something unique. Diversity sometimes leads to hardship, but it can also make you stronger.

Through adversity, Texans develop strength of character that communicates that they can handle just about anything. Like the state nickname and flag, Texas is a Lone Star among states. Texas doesn't want to be like any other state because Texans believe most things are just fine the way they are.

Big Tex. Library of Congress (LC-DIG-highsm-18725)

Resources

If you want to learn more about Texas's history, people, and culture, take a look at these books, websites, and places to visit.

Books

Cox, Mike. *Texas Ranger Tales: Stories That Need Telling*. Lanham, MD: Republic of Texas Press, 1997.

Dearen, Patrick. *Portraits of the Pecos Frontier* (revised). Lubbock: Texas Tech University Press, 1999.

Eisen, Jonathan, and Harold Straughn. *Unknown Texas*. New York: Macmillan Publishing Co., 1985.

Farlow, James O. *The Dinosaurs of Dinosaur Valley State Park*. Austin: Texas Parks and Wildlife, 1993.

Finsley, Charles E. *Discover Texas Dinosaurs*. Houston: Gulf Publishing Co., 1999.

Fisher, Lewis F. *The Spanish Missions of San Antonio*. San Antonio: Maverick Publishing, 1998.

Garrison, Walt, and Mark Stallard. *Then Landry Said to Staubach: The Best Dallas*

Cowboys Stories Ever Heard. Chicago: Triumph Books, 2007.

Greene, Casey Edward, and Shelly Henley Kelly (editors). *Through a Night of Horrors: Voices from the 1900 Galveston Storm*. Waco: Texas A&M University Press, 2000.

Life Magazine. *LIFE The Day Kennedy Died: 50 Years Later*. Alexandria, VA: Time Life Entertainment, Inc., 2013.

McComb, David G. *Texas: An Illustrated History*. New York: Oxford University Press, 1995.

Myers, John. *The Alamo*. Lincoln: University of Nebraska Press/Bison, 1973.

Oates, Stephen B. *Visions of Glory: Texans on the Southwestern Frontier*. Norman: University of Oklahoma Press, 1970.

Ramsay Jr., Jack C. *Jean Lafitte, Prince of Pirates*. Austin: Easkin Press, 1996.

Websites to Explore

Institute of Texan Cultures
www.texancultures.com
This website provides information about the brick-and-mortar museum, but there are plenty of extra features as well. Visitors can download publications about the history and effect of various cultures on Texas. There is also information about World War II. The site includes multimedia about the various types of housing found in Texas and about important African Americans in history.

New Perspectives on the West (PBS)
www.pbs.org/weta/thewest/program/
This website is supplemental to an eight-part television series. There is plenty here about the people of Texas, such as Stephen F. Austin and Álvar Núñez Cabeza de Vaca. Explore history with an interactive time line or primary source materials like diaries and letters.

San Jacinto Museum of History

www.sanjacinto-museum.org

THE SAN Jacinto Museum website lets you relive the battle that changed the course of history for Texas. You can read what led up to the battle, ponder Sam Houston's thinking, see what the battleground looked like, and view maps of other important areas.

Texas Beyond History

www.texasbeyondhistory.net

THIS WEBSITE created and maintained by the University of Texas at Austin bills itself as a virtual museum of Texas's culture heritage. Viewers can click on specific Texas map locations, explore geographic regions, or search for more information about the science of archeology.

Texas State Historical Association

www.tshaonline.org

THIS EXTENSIVE historical website covers Texas history from the dinosaurs to what happened yesterday. Readers can read popular articles or sign up for the RSS feed, Texas for a Day. Special features include African Americans, lighthouses in Texas, or the Kennedy assassination. New material is being added all the time.

Places to Visit

The Alamo

300 Alamo Plaza, San Antonio, TX 78516
(210) 225-1391
www.thealamo.org

THE SACRED shrine of the Alamo sits in the middle of San Antonio, drawing 2.5 million visitors a year from around the world. The 4.2-acre grounds, artifacts, and docents provide a vivid picture of what life must have been like when a small group of Texans, Tejanos, and frontiersmen held out for 13 days against the better armed and much larger Mexican army.

Dickens on the Strand

Downtown, Galveston, TX 77550
(409) 765-7424
www.galvestonhistory.org

EACH YEAR, Galveston holds a Victorian holiday street festival in the historic Strand district. People dressed in period costume stroll the streets, watching entertainment on one of five stages or buying gifts, food, and drink from costumed vendors. Often descendants of Charles Dickens attend as well. The tickets are half price for attendees wearing Victorian costumes.

Fort Worth Stockyards

500 NE 23rd Street, Fort Worth, TX 76164
(817) 624-4741
www.fortworthstockyards.org

THE FORT Worth Stockyards is a 98-acre historical and entertainment area near downtown Fort Worth. Concerts, restaurants, and shopping for real western gear are all available. But the highlight for many is the twice-daily cattle drives through the stockyard streets. Rodeos, cattle auctions, and special museum exhibits take place as well.

Panhandle-Plains Historical Museum

2503 4th Avenue, Canyon, TX 79015
(806) 651-2244
www.panhandleplains.org

TEXAS'S LARGEST history museum lets visitors not just see but also get a feeling of what life was like in Texas, whether it was with the dinosaurs, the Spanish explorers, or frontier life in Pioneer Town. You can also learn more about the oil industry. The Panhandle museum has everything you want to know about the Texas Panhandle and more.

San Antonio Missions National Historical Park

6701 San Jose Drive, San Antonio, TX 78214

(210) 534-8833

www.nps.gov/saan

San Antonio Missions National Historical Park is composed of four missions that operated long before Texas became a state—Mission Concepción, Mission San Jose, Mission San Juan, and Mission Espada. The missions all border the San Antonio River. Although all four have active churches, they are also much more; each is a complex that shows visitors what life was like during the mission days. An eight-mile hiking-biking trail connects the missions.

Sixth Floor Museum

411 Elm Street, Dallas, TX 75202

(214) 747-6660

www.jfk.org

Located in the old Texas Book Depository, the Sixth Floor Museum at Dealey Plaza chronicles the life, assassination, and legacy of President John F. Kennedy. Visitors are presented with photographs, artifacts, documentaries, and audio interviews as they trace Kennedy's life and death. The collection contains over 40,000 items.

Space Center Houston

1601 NASA Parkway, Houston, TX 77058

(281) 244-2100

www.spacecenter.org

Space Center Houston is affiliated with the Johnson Space Center and shows the past, present, and future of space travel through exhibits, hands-on activities, film, and special presentations. Visitors can see and talk to astronauts in the behind-the-scenes tour. For everyone who has ever wondered what it's like in space, Space Center Houston is a treat.

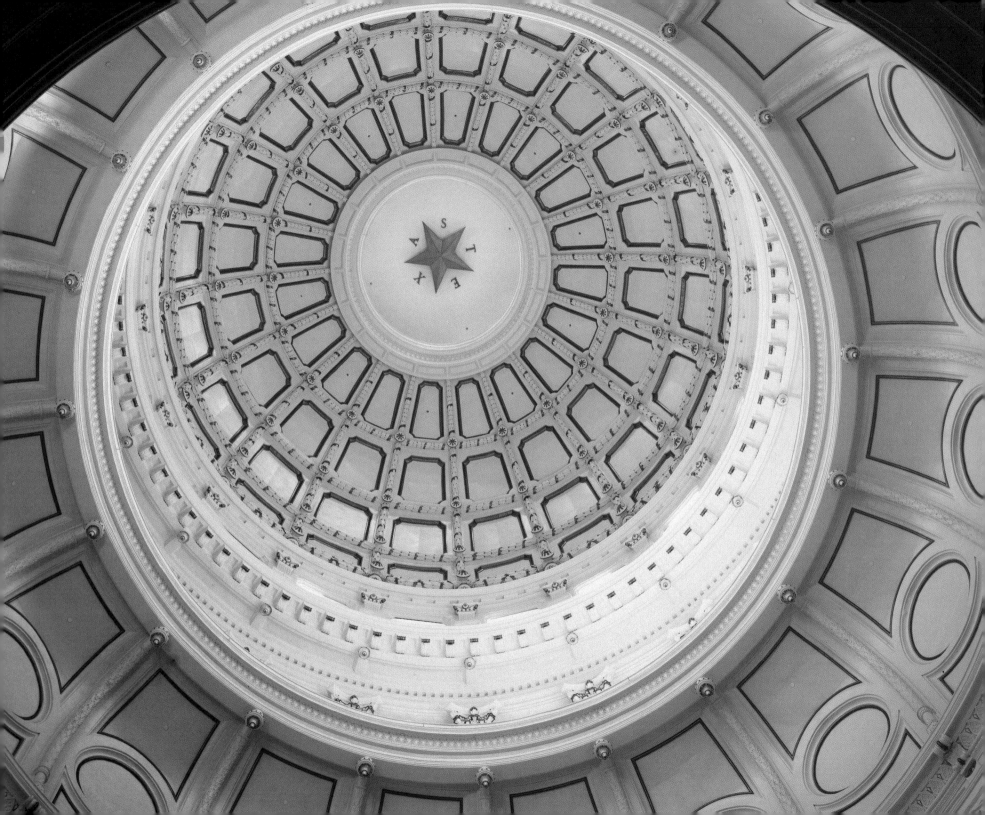

Index

Italicized page numbers indicate illustrations.

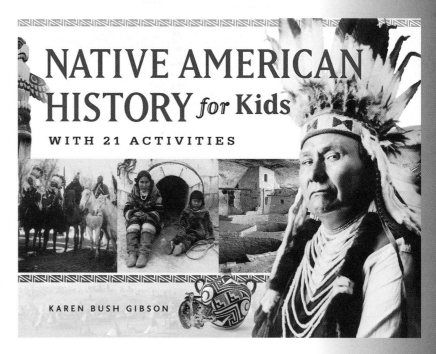